CO-OPERATIVE PRINCIPLES
TODAY & TOMORROW

The Author

William Pascoe Watkins BA, a former Director of the International Co-operative Alliance, is a leading authority on international Co-operation. Born in Plymouth, England, in 1893, son of a prominent local and national Co-operator, he trained as a schoolmaster and eventually became a tutor at the Co-operative College in 1920.

In 1929, Will Watkins joined the staff of the International Co-operative Alliance and in the next 10 years made his mark as a writer on Co-operative subjects. In 1939 he joined the Co-operative Sunday newspaper *Reynolds News*. In 1946 the British Government appointed him as Adviser on Co-operation to the Military Government of Western Germany to assist in the rehabilitation of the consumers' Co-operative Movement. Though his direct responsibilities ended with the formation of the Federal Republic in 1950, the German Co-operative Federations asked for his services for another year. In 1959, the Federal German Government conferred on him the Grand Cross of the Order of Merit in recognition of his services.

In 1951, he was appointed Director of the ICA and gave outstanding service to world Co-operation in that post until he retired in 1963. He has continued to be active as a writer, teacher and consultant on Co-operation, serving in 1965–66 as rapporteur of the ICA Commission on Co-operative Principles.

CO-OPERATIVE PRINCIPLES
TODAY & TOMORROW

W. P. WATKINS

With an introduction by
Professor T. F. Carbery

Holyoake Books
Manchester

Holyoake Books is the imprint
of the Co-operative Union Limited,
Holyoake House, Hanover Street,
Manchester M60 0AS

First published in May 1986

Reprinted 1990

Copyright © Co-operative Union Ltd 1986

British Library Cataloguing in Publication Data
Watkins, W.P.
   Co-operative principles : today and tomorrow
   1. Cooperative societies
   I. Title
   334   HD2963

ISBN 0 85195 140 6

Designed by Nick Horsfield
Typeset by Pen to Print, Colne, Lancashire BB8 9RS
Printed in Great Britain by Manchester Free Press

Contents

	Page
Preface	vii
Introduction	xi
CHAPTERS	
1 The Nature of Co-operative Principles	1
2 Association or Unity	18
3 Economy	36
4 Democracy	54
5 Equity	73
6 Liberty	92
7 Responsibility or Function	109
8 Education	123
9 Co-operative Principles and Social Progress	139
Notes	159
Index	164

Preface

The germinal idea of this study of the Principles of Co-operation goes back over 60 years to conversations with Thomas William Mercer, one of the most brilliant British exponents of Co-operation of this century, who was the writer's friend and his predecessor as tutor at the Co-operative College, then newly established in Manchester. The distinction, already implicit in the writing of Vansittart Neale,[1] the 19th century British Co-operative leader, between the Principles of Co-operation, which are universal ideas, and the rules, conventions and systems of organisation through which they are realised in any given set of circumstances, was clearly drawn by Mercer in these conversations. Some 10 years later he developed his thought in an article which appeared in the *Review of International Co-operation* in 1931 — the only place where his system of ideas, even though simply outlined, can now be found, formulated in his own words.

This article was contributed to the *Review* at the request of its Editor, Henry J. May,[2] who held that office in his capacity as General Secretary of the International Co-operative Alliance. He had been charged with the execution of a resolution, adopted the previous year by the International Co-operative Congress held in Vienna (1930), requiring the appointment of a special committee 'to inquire into the conditions under which the Rochdale Principles are applied in various countries and, if necessary, to define them'.

The resolution had been submitted in a short memorandum by the French National Federation of Consumers'

Co-operatives proposed by A. J. Cleuet who declared that the objects in view were three:

The first was to obtain a clear and complete list of the Principles of Rochdale.

The second, to ascertain how the principal rules of the Rochdale System were interpreted by the different national Co-operative Movements.

The third was to bring about agreement on the interpretation of the Principles under present-day economic conditions.

The Inquiry Committee was expected to report at the next Congress, which was to be held in London in 1933, but did not actually meet until 1934. Nor was its work finally accepted until Congress met again in Paris in 1937. Acceptance extended further to include amendments of the Rules of the ICA by the adoption of observance of the Principles of Rochdale, as formulated by the Committee, as the main condition for the admission of organisations claiming to be Co-operative to membership of the Alliance.

This provision remained in force until the second Vienna Congress in 1966. The faithful and steadfast enforcement of the Rules against persistent pressure became a principal factor in maintaining the unity of the Alliance in the third quarter of the present century. This stands out in contrast to those other international confederations which were irreparably split by political differences. More, it enabled the authorities of the Alliance to carry out a second inquiry into the Principles of Co-operation by a Special Commission, to correct the weaknesses of the earlier formulation, including therewith the amendment of the Rules, and secure their adoption by Congress, the supreme ICA authority, by overwhelming majorities.

After nearly 30 years, the need for revision of the Principles and Rules was becoming obvious to many Co-operators if by no means for the same reasons. Some Co-operators, convinced of the necessity of adjustment to a changing world, would wish to alter fundamentally the character and aims of the Movement, whereas others would want to resist any change whatever, because they fear the authority of the Principles may be diminished.

Neither of these extreme positions offers any hope of a solution, because they do not recognise the real problem, which is to ensure that the more Co-operation changes, the more it must remain the same thing — that it advances towards a more complete, not a more restricted, application of its Principles.

For this reason it was possible for the present writer (although convinced that Tom Mercer's approach was on the right lines), after rendering a little help to Henry May in his study of the Rochdale Principles, to accept the invitation of Gemmell Alexander (my successor as Director of the ICA) to serve as rapporteur of the Commission which reported in 1966. Each generation of Co-operators has to formulate its problems in its own terms and express its solutions in its own language.

The writer's debt, evident in every chapter, to the great French precursors and theorists of Co-operation and to eminent contemporary Co-operators, European and overseas, too numerous to name in a preface, is here gratefully acknowledged.

He also owes thanks beyond measure to a friend of long standing, the late Maurice Colombain, formerly Chief of the Co-operative Service of the International Labour Office, who read the first typescript and whose keen eye detected a number of omissions and obscurities in time for them to be corrected.

Nevertheless, the thanks of the author are due above all for the help and encouragement he has received from Peter Clarke, Research Officer of the Co-operative Party, and Roy Garratt, Librarian and Information Officer of the Co-operative Union. Without their interest and enthusiasm this book might well have remained just an unpublished typescript. Their criticism and suggestions for additions and omissions have resulted in great improvements in the book's actuality and clarity. It is no more than just that their invaluable contribution should be known to the reader.

That the book might well have been longer, with more ample treatment of many difficult questions, the writer willingly admits. But then, having passed four score years, he judged it unwise to plan a more ambitious work which, through failure of health or energy, he might not be able to finish. Moreover, as he hopes to be read by active Co-operators with limited time as well as by students and scholars by vocation, he does not wish to put them off by offering too bulky a volume. In any event, he never believed that, in order to say anything, it was necessary to say everything. If the lines of thought traced in these pages be found to lead in right directions, it is for younger Co-operators to pursue and extend them.

W. P. WATKINS

Long Compton
Warwickshire
January 1986

Introduction

'The International Co-operative Movement represents a great and inspiring idea of significance to the whole of mankind . . . Thus, Co-operation as a constructive expression of man's age-old instinct for mutual aid holds out hope. It offers men and women a clear unbroken line of thought and action, leading from association with their nearest neighbours and fellow workers stage by stage to mutual helpful relations with other men and women in the farthest corners of the world.'

That extract, quoted by J. H. Ollman, the former Editor of the Review of International Co-operation, is from *The International Co-operative Movement* by W. P. Watkins. That work gives an account of the world Movement, its size, its membership, its success — and its problems. Appropriately enough, it was published first in German, translated into Swedish and has subsequently appeared in English, Spanish and Japanese editions.

However, in this book the remarkable Will Watkins turns away from the descriptive to the world of theory and thought and unfolds with remarkable clarity of expression for such complex matters the inner workings of that same remarkable Movement — 'workings,' for as he makes abundantly clear, the Principles are the power-house of the Movement.

The author is himself, of course, remarkable. He was born in 1893. With a clear mind, a strong memory and a never-varying capacity for words he can recall, albeit not here, conversations with Co-operators and educationists such as W. R. Rae, Wilson Clayton and Albert Mansbridge, the founder of the Workers' Educational Association, and with Fred Hall, with whom he later collaborated to produce in 1935 — over 50 years ago — the much acclaimed, simply titled, *Co-operation*. Their acquaintance went back to before the First World War.

In 1909 he was one of a party which went to France to visit workers' and consumers' Co-operatives. The party was led by H. J. May who, 20 years later, when Secretary of the International Co-operative Alliance, invited the then young Will Watkins to join the Secretariat of that organisation. Yet later, in 1950, after work in Germany, he was destined to become Director of the ICA and so stand in apostolic succession to May.

In addition to knowledge, intelligence, intellectual curiosity, enthusiasm and a capacity for hard work, Will Watkins brought to the ICA an exceptional gift of tongues. Laurie Pavitt, the British Co-operative-Labour Member of Parliament, tells the story of how, having sent Will Watkins copies of the *Catalan Co-operative News*, he felt it incumbent on himself to inquire whether the recipient could read Catalan. 'Enough', he replied in his precise yet succinct manner. It then transpired that he had French and Spanish and thus, with his retained feeling for and knowledge of Latin, was able to follow the debates on the amendments of Co-operative Law in Barcelona. He has German, well-nigh perfected by his four years in Germany, and through German he is into the various Scandinavian languages.

In this work Will Watkins takes us to the heart of the matter — the Principles which make the Co-operative Movement tick, not merely here in Great Britain but throughout the international Co-operative Movement which he served so well. He makes it clear that the Principles did not emerge by way of spontaneous combustion or were not born exclusively from cerebral, intellectual debate. On the contrary, they were born out of reality, out of the experience of living.

More, they were destined to be endorsed by others in diverse lands and diverse economies.

And yet, there is a dilemma here which he does not shirk, for, if Co-operative Principles are born out of experience as well as philosophy, does that not imply, or oblige us to infer, that changing conditions inevitably give rise to changing, or at least modified, Principles?

This is important for, whereas he suggests an almost divine correlation between, on the one hand, adherence to these clearly enunciated Principles and commercial success and, on the other, the same connection between abandonment of these Principles leading to commercial failure, he does not shy from inviting attention to the situation when the choice lies between pristine adherence to these Principles or their development in order to prevail in the marketplace.

So, too, although the book is primarily about Principles, the author is much too realistic to overlook the significance of trade. It is trading, he reminds us, which gives the Principles, the theories, the underlying philosophy their reality. Moreover, in a delightfully gentle, *en passant* way he invites our attention, and particularly that of the British, to the strength of the commercially successful retail Co-operative in Dortmund in the Federal Republic of Germany.

Writing for the Society of Co-operative Studies, John Morley, the Chairman of the Plunkett Foundation, asked the question: 'What has made his (Watkins') views command attention?' He went on to proffer the answer: 'They are respected for several reasons, but principally because they represent the knowledge and experience of a man generally regarded as the best informed about the Co-operative situation in this country and overseas of all the men and women of his generation'. Not quite! Will Watkins is the best informed man on Co-operative matters in the world today: not only of his generation but the two which follow. Moreover, this book proves it!

T. F. CARBERY

University of Strathclyde
February 1986

CHAPTER ONE

The Nature of Co-operative Principles

> Par principes j'entends non les règles fixées par la coutume coopérative, mais les postulats moraux d'où ces règles dérivent. — Georges Fauquet.

> By principles I understand not the rules fixed by Co-operative custom, but the moral postulates whence these rules derive.

Today the term 'co-operation' and the adjective 'co-operative' enjoy a greater vogue than ever. Their increased use seems to have originated in the American branch of the English language and spread rapidly to the others, mainly because the use of English for international communication is becoming every year more extensive. The term, as it is commonly employed, denotes 'working together' in any manner whatever and therefore carries no precise meaning. When we employ it, as now, with an exact meaning and, in particular, to refer to a certain technique of working together, characteristic of a whole genus of economic and social organisations calling themselves 'co-operative' and now found all over the world, we need to write 'Co-operation' *with a capital C.*

This is the 'Co-operation' which is the subject of this book. Wherein does it differ from co-operation? In this way — that whereas co-operation stands for working together under any or no stipulated conditions, *Co-operation* denotes working together according to certain fundamental principles which those taking part agree to observe.

To define the essential Principles of Co-operation is no mere academic exercise. It presents itself as a practical problem, for example, to the legislator. As Co-operation spreads from country to country and governments appreciate its advantages as an element in their national economic systems, some form of legal provision has to be made for it, just as for any other type of association engaged in commerce, industry or banking. What kinds of association are to be recognised as Co-operatives by the law, given its protection, invested with legal personality and any further rights and privileges government may see fit to grant? A definition is indispensable, not only to mark off Co-operative association from any other types of economic association which work on different principles, but also to prevent bogus enterprises pretending to be Co-operative from enjoying the privileges intended for the genuine.

The very success of Co-operation and its extension around the world, the passage of time, and the inevitable tendency of institutions to ensure their own survival by coming to terms with their environment, conspire to increase the risk of its Principles being misunderstood, misinterpreted, diluted or even perverted. This was true at every period of the Co-operative Movement's long history. As the success of the Rochdale system of consumers' Co-operation became known in Europe more than 100 years ago, not a few societies were formed by would-be Co-operators who, failing to see that the system formed an integral whole, practised some Principles, while rejecting others and adding others still which the Pioneers did not practise. Those societies which did not realise their mistakes in time collapsed from a complex of causes: restricted membership, neglect of education, feeble democratic organs, credit trading, political and religious dissensions, besides general business inefficiency. At a later period the good reputation of Co-operation, especially among migrants from Europe to other continents, prompted unscrupulous individuals to foist on a too-confiding public self-styled co-operatives which were thinly-disguised private ventures, hardly distinguishable from rackets.

Co-operation is also liable to attract the attention of ambitious politicians or of political parties or religious organisations making totalitarian claims on the allegiance of their members. The Irishman who insisted in one of Horace Plunkett's[1] meetings that the dairy Co-operative then being promoted should manufacture butter on sound Nationalist principles has had his counterpart in many a country since, where the wine of emergent nationalism has temporarily blurred the people's vision. Where Co-operation is popular, the ambitious politician may be tempted to climb on its bandwagon but, in any case, Co-operation places power in the hands of the people, and parties may be either jealous of that power in itself or apprehensive of it becoming affected to other parties. Where there exists a close personal connection between Co-operative Movements and political parties there is always a risk of pressure on Co-operatives to compromise with their Principles for party ends and, in these days of centrally-planned economic development, of Co-operative Movements being diverted from their natural or normal line of advance in order to discharge functions determined, not by their members seeking to meet their own needs, but by the aims and doctrines of the political party in power.

This was the nub of the controversy which divided the International Co-operative Alliance after the Russian Revolution of 1917 and which became acute in the 1940's after Communist governments had been set up in other European countries following the westward advance of the Soviet armed forces. Two mutually inconsistent arguments were advanced from the Communist side. The first is that in Communist countries Co-operatives are permitted and continue to practise the true Principles of Rochdale in conformity with the conditions laid down by the ICA for affiliation. The second is that the Principles as formulated or interpreted by the authorities of the Alliance are out of date in the 20th century and therefore constitute an obstacle to the unity of the Co-operative Movement on a world-wide basis. They ought therefore to be revised and reformulated in terms, not of the laisser faire economic policies of a century ago, but of the regulated and planned economies of the present day. This argument is to be found in the memorandum submitted by Centrosoyus (the Central Union of Consumer Co-operative Societies) of the USSR to the 22nd Congress of the ICA at Bournemouth in 1963 to support a resolution, eventually adopted with amendments, in favour of a re-examination of Co-operative Principles. Hitherto, the reply of the authorities of the Alliance had been first, that the Principles of Rochdale were as valid then as ever they were and, second, that they were not adequately observed by the organisations called Co-operatives in Communist countries.

Yet another factor of confusion about Co-operative Principles, possibly more potent and of longer duration than those already mentioned, is the daily wear and tear of maintaining the Co-operative position in fiercely competitive markets. Never was this competition more severe than it is today for the old-established Co-operative organisations of Europe and North America. The temptation to sacrifice considerations of principle to the need to counter the aggressive methods of competitors by turning their own weapons against them, grows stronger — all the more so where Co-operative managers and administrators, even if proficient in business techniques, are insufficiently grounded in Co-operative Principles and therefore do not really understand the nature of the institution they serve or how to turn the Movement's basic ideas to competitive advantage.

This temptation was, of course, always latent in the competitive situation of the Co-operative Movement, especially as its material success became assured, its commitments increased and its pioneering era receded into the past. The maintenance and development of established institutions inevitably becomes an end in itself, obscuring the ultimate purpose for which the institutions were created, while the principles on which they were founded are obscured by gloss upon gloss, expedient upon expedient. In the 1920's, the then General Secretary of the International Co-operative Alliance, Henry J. May, began to call attention to the dangers inherent in this tendency and in the extent to which departures from accepted principles were being tolerated or even advocated in more than one country. The Congress of the ICA in Vienna in 1930 accordingly resolved that the Alliance should carry out an inquiry among its members into the present application of the Rochdale Principles. For this purpose a special committee was appointed which reported to the Congresses of 1934 and 1937. Its reports were approved and, as a result of its recommendations, certain amendments were made to the Rules of the Alliance designed to ensure that only those organisations were admitted to membership which conformed, in their constitution and modes of operation, to the Rochdale Principles.

This first ICA inquiry preluded a period of swift, kaleidoscopic changes in economic and social conditions, as well as in the political map of the world. In this period the Co-operative Movement achieved world-wide extension, with a notable growth in the non-European membership of the Alliance in consequence. If this ever more diversified membership of the Alliance is to be held together, if the necessary help for Co-operative development is to be provided in the right fraternal spirit from country to country and continent to continent, if the opportunities of inter-trading and mutual economic support in other ways are to be seized and turned to advantage, then Co-operators of all countries must be clear in their minds about the Principles which they hold in common and which determine the character of Co-operation and the differences between it and State economic organisations, on the one hand, and all kinds of profit enterprise on the other.

In an earlier paragraph, Co-operation was described as working together according to certain principles which those taking part agree to observe. Unfortunately, the word 'principle' has different meanings for different people. Almost anything may become a matter of principle if anyone is not willing to compromise upon it. The first ICA inquiry encountered this difficulty, for before it could deal with its proper subject, namely, the application of the Rochdale Principles, it had to determine what the Rochdale Principles were — and were not. In fact it accepted some pretended principles and rejected others, stating its reasons in its report. In contrast to the editor of Häntschke's German translation of G. J. Holyoake's[2] *History of the Rochdale*

Pioneers, who enumerated no less than 15 Principles, the ICA Inquiry Committee declared the following seven features of the Rochdale system to be really essential and therefore to be regarded as Principles:

1. Open and voluntary membership.
2. Democratic control — one member, one vote.
3. Limited interest on capital.
4. Dividend on purchases.
5. Neutrality in politics and religion.
6. Cash payments in buying and selling.
7. Promotion of education.

Nevertheless, the Committee drew a distinction between the first four and the last three items on this list. It was considered that the adoption and practice of the first four are essential to the maintenance of the Co-operative character of any society or organisation. It may be observed that, although the Committee was studying the rules and practice of the Rochdale Pioneers' Society, which was a consumers' society, it was really in search of the Principles which would apply to Co-operative societies universally and which would accordingly define the character of the whole Co-operative genus. Incidentally, conformity to the first four, sometimes in a slightly modified formulation, is required today of every organisation applying for affiliation to the International Co-operative Alliance as evidence of its genuinely Co-operative character. In the case of producers' Co-operative marketing organisations, for example, dividend would require to be calculated on the basis of sales, not purchases.

In regard to the last three Principles, however, the ICA Committee was obliged to admit that they — in its own words — 'while undoubtedly part of the Rochdale system, may be regarded as essential methods of action and organisation, rather than standards, the non-observance of which would destroy the Co-operative character of the society'. The distinction drawn by the Committee between 'methods' and 'standards' seems to be valid in one sense, but not in another. It can hardly be denied that the first four Principles are absolutely vital to the Co-operative character of any society or federation. All the same, they are just as much 'methods' as the other three. In fact, all seven would probably be more properly termed *practical rules* which, if faithfully and efficiently carried out, ensure that a society will preserve its Co-operative character and, if not make a success of its business, at least avoid some of the commonest causes of failure.

A Commission of five members, three from Europe and one from America who unanimously chose the fifth — an Indian — as their Chairman, was appointed by the ICA Congress of Bournemouth in 1963 to carry out the second inquiry into the observance of the Rochdale Principles. It took as its starting point the final report of the first inquiry which had been accepted by the Paris Congress of 1937. The Commission, working against the background of a greatly expanded International Co-operative Alliance and a vastly altered world economic and political situation, had much wider scope for research and immeasurably more assistance and collaboration from the ICA's affiliated organisations, even though its aims were substantially the same as those of the earlier Committee. The Commission did in fact recognise the historical continuity in the search for truth and clarity in defining Co-operative Principles which link the precursors of Co-operation, who anticipated the Rochdale Pioneers, with those who today are endeavouring to realise the Co-operative idea in regions in the early stages of economic development. The Commission declared that its task proved to be one of 'clearing up confusion and removing unnecessary rigidity rooted in unbalanced or over-simplified interpretations, a process of refurbishing which permits the underlying Principles to shine with a brighter light'. It also emphasised that Co-operation's aims extend beyond the promotion of economic interests of individual Co-operators to contributions to moral and social values. These justify it being tested from this standpoint, as well as from that of business efficiency.

The Commission's final formulation, which was not only approved by the Vienna Congress of 1966 but also in part incorporated in ICA Rules laying down conditions for the admission of new members and the retention of their membership, was as follows:

1. Membership of a Co-operative society should be voluntary and available without artificial restriction or any social, political, racial or religious discriminations, to all persons who can make use of its services and are willing to accept the responsibilities of membership.
2. Co-operative societies are democratic organisations. Their affairs should be administered by persons elected or appointed in a manner agreed by the members and accountable to them. Members of primary societies should enjoy equal rights of voting (one member, one vote) and participation in decisions affecting their societies. In other than primary societies the administration should be conducted on a democratic basis in a suitable form.
3. Share capital should only receive a strictly limited rate of interest, if any.
4. Surplus or savings, if any, arising out of the operations of a society belong to the members of that society and should be distributed in such manner as would avoid one member gaining at the expense of others.
   This may be done by decision of the members as follows —
   (a) By provision for development of the business of the Co-operative;
   (b) By provision of common services; or
   (c) By distribution among the members in proportion to their transactions with the society.
5. All Co-operative societies should make provision for the education of their members, officers, and employees and of the general public, in the principles and techniques of Co-operation, both economic and democratic.
6. All Co-operative organisations, in order to best serve the interests of their members and their communities, should actively co-operate in every practical way with other Co-operatives at local, national and international levels.

Comparison of the above text with the Committee's list submitted in 1934 reveals how much had been gained in clarity and precision. The Commission emphasised the universality of the Principles; they were to be observed by all genuine Co-operatives at all times. It had given greater precision to such concepts as 'open' membership and 'neutrality' in a political and religious context. It limited interest payment to share capital only, while allowing greater freedom in the allocation of surplus to benefit individual members or social purposes. Nor would it accept the 1934 Committee's idea of obligatory and non-obligatory Principles — 'No distinction of degree of validity can be drawn between essential Principles'. Co-operative education should extend beyond actual Co-operative membership to the general public. And it declared that co-operation between Co-operatives for the benefit of their members and the community at large was a Principle to be observed at local, national and international levels.

What the Commission did not do was make clear the distinction between Principles and practices. It rather tended to confuse them by defining Co-operative Principles 'as those practices which are essential, that is absolutely indispensable to the achievement of the Co-operative Movement's purpose'. In the last analysis the proof of any society's or federation's fidelity to Co-operative Principles is its practice. Yet a distinction may justly be drawn between rules and practices on the one hand and Principles on the other. The rules and practices, which may be conventions and usages as well as strict and precise formulations in a society's statutes, are the methods by which the Principles are carried into effect. They are bound to vary according to times and circumstances. In recent years, consumer Co-operatives have found it practically inexpedient under contemporary trading, if not impracticable, to adhere rigidly to the Rochdale rule of cash payments. Or again, the rule of 'one member, one vote', which is indispensable to the practice of democracy in primary Co-operatives consisting of individuals, may be an absurdity when applied to unions or federations which have a membership consisting of societies differing widely in size. Insistence on this rule in the Finnish Co-operative Union (SOK) was one of the factors contributing to the split in 1917, when a large group of societies seceded to form the KK Union. With the passage of time, the old resentments have been appeased, but the two organisations remain apart to this day. In contrast to the practical rules, however, the Principles which inform and justify them remain invariable. The Co-operative philosopher Dr G. Fauquet[3] was fully aware of this when he pleaded, in the International Co-operative Congress of 1934, that the delegates should not attach as much — or even more — importance to formal regulations as to the general Principles which he called 'postulates' which form the foundation of the Movement.

It is the general Principles, the elements in Co-operation which are constant in all times and places, which constitute the true object of present study. The seven points of the Rochdale System enumerated by the ICA Committee, in so far as they are methods, are means and not ends in themselves. They derive their validity and authority from the ends which they serve, that is to say, the ultimate values and verities on which the concept of Co-operation reposes. It is a mistake, which only adds to confusion, to call Co-operation itself a Principle. Neither as idea nor as practice is it a simple, primordial, elementary thing. It belongs to the category of methods, techniques and systems. It owes its existence to the urge to develop an art of social organisation satisfying and reconciling certain vital human needs which are different, often divergent and may even be, in some degree and under particular conditions, conflicting. In the search, therefore, for the primary elements of the Co-operative idea we are obliged to take a different line of approach from that taken by the ICA inquiries embarking on this task. However, it is indispensable to emphasise their positive achievements.

Starting our inquiry afresh, it seems reasonable to seek the elements of the Co-operative idea in certain fundamental and universal facts or situations of human nature and experience.

First, there is man himself, a social animal, gregarious, living in communities, dependent on his fellow-man, not only for physical survival but also for spiritual stimulus and growth. Association is instinctive but it is also deliberate because of its advantages, expressed universally in the proverb 'Union is strength' and its many variants.

Second, there is the condition of man's continued existence on this planet: labour to produce and distribute the necessities of physical and intellectual life. It is through measuring the results of their labour against the efforts and sacrifices required to obtain them that men learn to manage their resources and so evolve the idea of Economy. From the union of Association and Economy springs division of labour, that inexhaustible source of material benefits and higher standards of living.

Third, what men produce by their combined labour must necessarily be distributed. If production be social, most consumption cannot help being individual. Distribution, however, must not simply satisfy men's wants, but also their moral sense by being fair, just and equitable, taking into account individual contributions as well as individual needs.

Fourth, if men's combined labours are to be efficient and fruitful, they must be well organised and directed. Organisation demands a system of government, an accepted authority for making and executing decisions on what shall be done and how it shall be done. In modern times, in all sorts of associations, the tendency is for those who exercise authority to be answerable to the whole body of those for and over whom it is exercised or, in other words, for government to be more or less democratic.

Fifth, there is man's unquenchable aspiration to be free. Though he is dependent on his neighbours, he also desires to be, as far as possible, independent of them, in order to be himself and to fulfil himself in his own way. In any event, he gives of his best only when he devotes his energy to what he freely undertakes, when his participation in combined effort is not compulsory but voluntary — in short, when his will is engaged.

Sixth, man's life is one of continual adaptation — to his own changing needs, as he grows through childhood and youth into old-age, and to the social order around him. The life of human societies, their security and well-being attain a high level only when men are enlightened enough to direct the forces of nature and to accept the need of order and discipline in their mutual relations. Education, including re-education, in this sense is indispensable to social stability, welfare and progress.

These elementary facts or needs form part of universal human experience. For that reason they themselves, or ideas to which they directly give rise, are accepted in varying degrees everywhere as guides to social policy or institutional development. Any economic or political system, if it is to achieve stability and endure and, at the same time, if it is to remain open to possibilities of progress, must come to terms with them. The Rochdale Pioneers recognised this. It says much for their penetration into social realities that, in their celebrated 'Law First' of their Society's Rules, which set forth their immediate and ultimate aims, they stated that they would need to 'arrange the powers of production, distribution, education and government' in order to establish the self-supporting, united community of their dreams. But what was true of their ideal community was no less true of the business enterprise which was their immediate objective, and there is no ground for supposing that the same insight did not inspire the drafting of its rules — an insight which had been sharpened by the struggle to live and bring up families decently on slender means and, in times of slack employment, actual want.

The Principles and general ideas embodied in the Rules of the Pioneers' Society were not the outcome of any man's wishful dreaming but the product of reflection upon experience, confirmed by the test of critical discussion over the better part of two years. What is remarkable, significant and indeed conclusive for the present argument is that the practice and underlying ideas of the Rochdale Pioneers were subjected to the test, not only of discussion, but also of the hard realities of business life for over a century and were confirmed again and again both positively and negatively. Positively, where the Rochdale practice was adopted (not slavishly copied, but applied with understanding of the fundamental ideas), consumers' Co-operative societies had the best chance of survival as business undertakings against competitive conditions, without sacrificing in any important respect what may be called, for want of a better term, the spirit of Co-operation. Negatively, rejection of the Rochdale system, or of any important feature of its practice, was repeatedly proved to be the surest way to failure in business, as well as degeneration in a Co-operative sense.

No less significant is the independent growth of the agricultural Co-operative Movement, for agricultural Co-operators, working in other lands within a different background of experience and with other objectives in view, arrived at a body of principles identical in all essentials with the Rochdale System. Or again, in the late 1880's it was not difficult for Horace Plunkett, having decided that Ireland's need was for agricultural rather than consumers' Co-operation, to draft the rules of his first dairy society using the Co-operative Union's model rules for consumers' societies as a basis.

It is perhaps now possible to sum up the argument by elaborating our previous definition of Co-operative Principles. Co-operative Principles are the general ideas which inspire and govern the application of the Co-operative technique of social organisation. These ideas result from inductive reasoning upon experience of fundamental and universal social realities. They lay down lines for the Co-operative solution of social problems to which those realities give rise. The Principles are common to all forms of Co-operation in all times and places. Their effective observance is the test of the genuineness of Co-operative institutions and a guarantee of sound and efficient Co-operative practice. Corresponding to the six social facts enumerated earlier there are six Co-operative Principles, as follows:

Association (or Unity); Economy; Equity; Democracy; Liberty; Education.

Later chapters will discuss each Principle separately, as well as a seventh: Function (or Responsibility) which has hitherto remained implicit in the Co-operative System rather than explicitly stated, still less examined. There are, however, certain general observations applicable to all the Principles which can be most usefully made in the present chapter.

What is the authority of the Co-operative Principles just enumerated? From what do they derive their validity and possibly binding force? Before attempting to answer these questions, it should first be emphasised that they do not derive their authority from any individual, be he visionary, prophet or teacher. It is not that many social prophets and teachers have not in the past thrown light on the Principles or called attention in an impressive way to the value and importance of Co-operation. But it is a commonplace of the Movement's history that in Great Britain the common people — the weavers of Fenwick in Ayrshire and the dockyard workers in Woolwich — were experimenting with Co-operative methods long before Robert Owen[4] expounded his 'New View of Society', just as in other countries they were groping their way towards Co-operation before they learned of Fourier's[5] *phalanstery* or the success of the Rochdale Pioneers. The validity of Co-operative Principles is founded upon the experience and common sense of the many, not on a revelation made to or by a few. In the words of Charles Gide,[6] 'Co-operation springs from the very bowels of the people.'

The basis of Co-operative Principles and their practical application alike stand the test of scientific analysis. As previously indicated, their definition has been reached by a process which is essentially inductive and, as general propositions, they can claim the same kind of validity in their sphere as economic or sociological principles possess in their respective sciences. If they possess a similar authority, they are also subject to the same relativity. In other words, they are liable to revision and re-formulation in the light of fresh experience. Indeed, if they are to serve the need of Co-operative action for inspiration and guidance, and if the Movement is to preserve its dynamism, they must be re-examined and re-interpreted by each successive generation, as their practical application is demanded in novel forms in a rapidly evolving world.

But if the Principles can claim an authority which is truly scientific, they also derive authority from a source which may be called pragmatic: the Co-operative Movement lives and grows, not through its theoretical rightness or consistency, but by its superiority in achieving practical ends. For that reason, for many of its members and leaders, Co-operative truth is what works. If we reject such a view as an over-simplification and as leading in the long run to an ever-narrowing concept of Co-operative aims and practice, we are bound nevertheless to admit that the authority of Co-operative Principles is enhanced and reinforced by the successful demonstration of their possibilities of application, both in the past and in the present and future also.

The aims of the Movement are achieved, in short, not when it proves theorems but when it solves problems.

The third source from which Co-operative Principles derive their authority, although not all to the same degree, is ethical. One of them, Equity, is essentially ethical, but the manner in which some of the others rest upon ethical considerations and take on the character of moral obligations can perhaps be illustrated by reference to another principle, namely Association. As a Co-operative Principle, Association rests primarily upon the massive fact of human solidarity. Bemused as we often are by what some Hindu philosophers would call the illusion of separateness, few of us realise, until we read such a book as Charles Gide's *La Solidarité*, what a pervasive, dominating and inescapable fact solidarity is and always has been in the life of mankind. To recognise and act upon it brings its own reward; just as to ignore or defy it brings its own punishment by natural consequences. The Co-operative Principle of Association goes, of course, much farther than mere recognition of the fact of man's community and mutuality of interests. It implies that Co-operators not only accept the associations — family, community, nation — into which they are born, but also seek other associations deliberately and purposefully for the sake of the material and spiritual advantages they offer and, above all, for the power they confer on the associates so long as they remain united.

But beyond this again, when we recognise — and who can fail to do so? — how swiftly contemporary means of communication and transport, coupled with international division of commerce and industry, are linking and binding together the remotest peoples as never before in history, so that traditional self-sufficiency and individualism are clearly seen to be not simply impracticable as either private conduct or public policy, but also positively harmful as a menace to security and a hindrance to the spread of well-being throughout the world, then the Principle of Association acquires moral as well as scientific and pragmatic authority. In other words, it embodies for Co-operators and others besides a moral obligation, a duty to be fulfilled towards their fellow-men. Of course, the fact that Co-operative Principles have an ethical content does not link Co-operation with any particular moral philosophy or definition of the ultimate good, such as Happiness or the fulfilment of Duty. Nevertheless it does explain why Co-operators of the various continents find sanctions for the practice of Co-operation in the teaching of human brotherhood or good neighbourliness common to the different world religions or outlook they individually profess.

If it be objected that neither Association nor any other of the Principles here discussed is peculiar to Co-operation and that the Co-operative Movement cannot make any exclusive claim to principles which obtain more or less widespread acceptance and application in the world at large, two observations may be made. Co-operators are fully aware, none more so, that the capitalist system, as it evolved, tended to abandon the cruder kinds of individualism and make constantly greater use of the Principle of Association. The rings, cartels and trusts which Co-operative organisations consistently oppose are the outcome of processes of horizontal and vertical integration not unlike, in certain respects, those which the Co-operative Movement itself employs in the course of its development. Another striking example is the speed with which in the 1950's the smaller retailers in several countries banded themselves together in voluntary chains and even established international connections, in order to counterbalance the advantages enjoyed by their mammoth competitors, the supermarket companies.

Moreover, so far as the Principle of Democracy is concerned, the Co-operative Movement is one of a large family of people's movements which includes the trade unions, the mutual benefit societies and many kinds of voluntary association, all democratic in constitution and spirit.

Co-operators never claimed to have discovered or invented these Principles but merely to apply them consistently to the promotion of social welfare. Driven by hardship, insecurity, oppression and injustice to examine the fundamental realities of society and to build a better social system than that under which they suffered, they selected Principles which they found to be applied in the world at large in a limited and haphazard manner, often in conflict with one another. Their criticism of contemporary capitalism, for example, was — to use our present vocabulary — that it pursued Economy with no regard or respect for Equity, Democracy or Liberty. It permitted the distribution of the social product to be determined by those with the greatest bargaining power in the market. It suppressed the self-direction of the craftsmen and replaced it by autocracy in the workshop and slavery to machines, even though it may have grudgingly tolerated some approach to democracy in civic and political life. That economic progress has been made and social welfare enhanced under capitalist auspices it would be idle to deny, but against these gains there is a heavy debt of human deprivation, misery, insecurity, and international and social strife.

On the other hand, the merit of the Co-operative Movement and what is in fact peculiar to it is the co-ordination and balancing of fundamental Principles in institutions and practices tending to maximise social welfare. Its supreme virtue is its capacity for concentrating in action year in year out, so much that the consensus of men and women, irrespective of race or creed, can accept as right and good. This is the virtue which has enabled Co-operation in a century and a half to spread out from Europe to the ends of the earth and which justifies its aspiration to become universal, not merely in extent, but also through its application intensively, in the Owenite phrase, to 'every purpose of social life'. Human fallibility will always ensure that Co-operative practice has its limitations and imperfections, but so long as the Movement effectively applies its Principle of Education, the possibility remains that it will approach indefinitely the perfection which is its proper end.

CHAPTER TWO

Association or Unity

The Principle discussed in this chapter appears under two names for no other reason than that it is often more convenient to use one rather than the other, according to the context. Association is perhaps more appropriate in considering the origins and early stages of Co-operative Movements everywhere, that is, the coming together of persons or social groups hitherto standing apart or mutually independent. Unity, on the other hand, seems the handier term when discussing, as this chapter will do before it concludes, the structures and policies of Co-operative organisations. At all times, however, the meaning is the same; the idea of individuals or entities joining together, coalescing, combining, integrating and remaining united in order to satisfy common needs, achieve common ends, or derive mutual advantage from their association.

Nor need it be any occasion for stumbling at the outset that the ICA Committee of 1930–37 should not have included Association in its list of Rochdale Principles or that the Pioneers themselves said little about it. Both parties were so deeply committed to it that they took it for granted. Much more important is the fact that the Pioneers not merely practised association within their own society, but also applied it, in conjunction with neighbouring societies, in solving some of the most vital of their problems, notably wholesale purchase and supply. Least of any, however, should the present generation of Co-operators take the Principle of Unity for granted or regard it as too obvious to need discussion. More than a century of Co-operative practice since the Pioneers has served only to enhance the importance of the Principle and its role in Co-operative policy and structural development on all levels, from the local to the international. Some of the most difficult, not to say desperate, problems now confronting the older national Co-operative Movements threaten to prove intractable, largely because the Principle of Unity has not been sufficiently appreciated and discussed — and in consequence, understood and intelligently applied. Contrary to the opinion expressed by certain authorities, who regard Democracy as the fundamental Co-operative Principle, the present writer holds that Unity is the most vital of the seven. Unity is the source of whatever power any Co-operative Movement acquires or wields. Its maintenance is the indispensable condition of the effective observance of the other six Principles — its impairment or propagation in false forms or on wrong bases is the worst injury that can be inflicted on the Movement. It carries an overriding authority to which all the other Principles may all be obliged in the last resort to defer and it has therefore been taken first for individual examination in the present work.

Significantly, if somewhat late in the day, the Principle, in the guise of 'Co-operation between Co-operatives', was recognised by the ICA Special Commission of the 1960's. It appears last in the Commission's list because it was considered after the list in the 1937 Report had been examined and amended. Its adoption was proposed by Howard A. Cowden, who had himself played a leading role in the evolution of the Consumers' Co-operative Association into Farmland Industries in the USA and the establishment of the International Co-operative Petroleum Association. Cowden declared that he had been mandated to put forward his proposal by the Co-operative League of the USA. He had not the slightest difficulty in securing ready acceptance by the other four members of the Commission and their collaboration in its final formulation which was in due course adopted by the second Vienna Congress in 1966.

Historically, the need for conscious affirmation of Association as a doctrine arose from the fact that, when the Industrial Revolution of the 18th and 19th centuries broke over Europe, the social nature of man was insufficiently realised or understood. Economic science was in its infancy, but unfortunately was taken as revealing more truth than it had in fact discovered. Other social sciences, which might have corrected or modified the doctrines of the economists and their over-simplifying popularisers and which in time actually did so, were not then existent. The very fact of society seemed to vanish from the minds of men dazzled by new technical inventions and their promise of unlimited riches. But if the sciences did not yet exist, the facts were there — the competitive struggle for wealth and the consequences of covetousness and ignorance, the exploitation, degradation and misery of the economically weaker, trodden underfoot in the struggle for a livelihood. The 20th century parallel of this atomised society may now be seen in the great seaports, industrial centres and mining settlements of the newly-developing countries, where the new proletariat, created by the impact of modern economic organisation on ancient ways of life, is to be found.

No countervailing or remedial action could be expected without a powerful assertion of the truth of solidarity and the value of Association in the face of the prevailing individualist orthodoxy. That was the life's work of Robert Owen. At New Lanark Owen tried, with a great measure of success, to weld into a community the assorted collection of rootless, immigrant workers and their families who had gravitated there in search of employment and who depended for their livelihood on his mill. After he left there he went on throughout his long life preaching community, Co-operation, socialism, whatever was fashionable at any time — in other words affirming the necessity of Association for normal, balanced, healthy, human life. It was Owen's preaching which gave inspiration and direction to the instinctive mutual aid among British working people already taking shape in their trade unions, mutual benefit and Co-operative societies. From the marriage of Owen's community idea with working-class good neighbourliness and common sense sprang the Co-operative Movement in Great Britain.

While the debate about competition and society continued in time and widened in space with the extension of machine industry and the factory system, Owen's community idea and, more particularly, its practical realisation were expounded in England by William Thompson[1] and Dr William King.[2] In contemporary France the ideas of Saint-Simon,[3] who prophesied an age of organisation, of Fourier, one of a number who projected ideal communities, of Buchez,[4] who advocated self-governing workshops, contained formidable criticism of the competitive market economy and set the minds of many thoughtful men on the track of Association and Co-operation as constructive alternatives. In Germany the plight of the handicraftsmen and peasants during 'the hungry 40's' moved Hermann Schulze-Delitzsch[5] and Friedrich Wilhelm Raiffeisen[6] to attempt practical organisation tending in the same direction.

If in the middle of the 19th century competition appeared to gain somewhat in scientific authority from popular oversimplification of Darwin's evolutionary theories, Association later gained even more from the studies of the Russian social philosopher Peter Kropotkin who not only demonstrated the role of mutual aid in animal and human society and the evolution of man's moral qualities, but also revealed the new opportunities for associated labour offered by modern technology. From the middle of the 19th century the pendulum began to swing back from extreme individualism. In the half-century between 1840 and 1890 the four basic types of Co-operative (the consumers' society, the workers' productive society, the credit society, urban and rural, and the farmers' marketing and processing society) had been worked out and in a number of European countries had demonstrated their value and their ability to survive. The argument for unlimited competition went by the board when capitalist industry itself recoiled from it and sought refuge in collusion through the familiar forms of vertical and horizontal combination which are all-pervasive today.

The primary objective of Co-operative associations, whether their founders or members do or do not dream of far-reaching social consequences, is normally to obtain power over the nearest part of the economic mechanism on which their livelihood or standard of living depends. They associate in order to perform the functions of ownership, organisation, direction and risk-bearing ordinarily discharged in a market economy by individuals or groups of entrepreneurs. Urban consumers set up retail shops, urban artisans people's banks, industrial wage-earners workers' productive societies, peasants or farmers rural credit or agricultural supply, marketing and processing societies, and so on. The various economic advantages they thereby secure are reserved for discussion in the chapter on Economy. The important feature for our present purpose is that Co-operative societies of whatever kind are mechanisms for the generation and employment of economic power, which is mostly out of their members' reach as individuals. In a market economy, the simplest form of this power is bargaining-power which the associates may exercise as either buyers or sellers. The bargaining, i.e. purchasing power of a single consumer, even if he or she buys for a large family, may be negligible; the purchasing power of a thousand in a local market will probably be appreciable. The purchasing power of a hundred thousand can dominate the retail market of a big city, that of a million can influence a nationwide market, when they concentrate it in the hands of a single buying organisation.

This bargaining power is, of course, not dissimilar in kind to that exercised by trade unions in the labour market. However, in order to be effective, it needs to be exerted in a rather different manner. Consumers' strikes are not unknown, but experience suggests that consumers' purchasing power yields more satisfying results when it is not expended in spasmodic actions, but embodied in permanent institutions of which the Co-operative society is one of the most important. In principle, Association tends to lighten the burden of competition resting on the individual consumer or producer, and may often shift the balance of competition from one to the other side of the market. In the marketing of certain kinds of agricultural produce, Association enables the peasant with produce to sell to cease going in search of a buyer and may compel the buyers to come to the Co-operative in search of the product. This is the effect of the system of sale by auction adopted in Holland by the Co-operatives of vegetable, fruit and flower growers, in whose warehouses the buyers may be seen bidding against one another by pushing a button, while a rotating pointer passes over the price-figures painted on a large dial.

Association confers power on the economically powerless by providing them with a means of making their numbers tell. Other things being equal, that is assuming competence in organisation and business policy, the greater the numbers, the greater the power and the greater the benefits to be shared. Co-operative associations are therefore almost invariably open associations, membership in which is deliberately kept open to all who have a use for the services which the associations provide. In the case of consumers, interested in purchasing the necessities of life, the application is obvious and the tendency, as consumers' Co-operative Movements grow, is to make entry easier by reducing to a minimum the formalities of registration and the down-payment required. For example, shares are often paid, up to the minimum holding prescribed in the rules, not in cash, but by the retention by the society of part of the dividend due to the member on his or her purchases. For obvious reasons the societies normally reserve the right to protect themselves against notoriously bad characters or persons likely to cause disruption, but in the normal way the rule of open membership is applied without discrimination.

The case of certain of the producers' societies is somewhat different. Most of the services provided by agricultural Co-operatives are of interest only to farmers or cultivators, but it is nevertheless often observable that membership of credit or supply societies is open to any member of the rural community.

The most difficult case is probably that of the workers' Co-operative productive or labour contracting society, membership of which can be affected one way or another by the employment situation. If business is booming such societies may be obliged to engage supplementary or auxiliary workers in order to fulfil their contracts, but they will never grant their workers full membership rights until they have had an opportunity of proving in the factory or other workplace that they are technically competent, of good character and likely to take seriously their responsibilities as members if they are admitted. On the other hand, in industries which absorb a high proportion of juvenile labour, particularly young girls who expect to give up their employment on getting married or soon afterwards, workers' productive societies have encountered great difficulty in persuading workers to apply for full membership.

To sum up, it may be said that, while certain practical limitations on the practice of open membership, dictated by common sense in the light of external circumstances, are admissible, the Principle of Association is violated when any Co-operative society refuses admission to membership in order to restrict the enjoyment of its benefits to a limited circle.

Association does not confer bargaining power alone. Societies which are so efficiently managed as to maintain their position in the market and also expand enable their members to acquire economic power in other ways. Successful Co-operatives make for their members both collective and individual savings, which may be employed as capital for their common advantage. The members acquire individual savings through sharing in their society's trading surplus in proportion to the volume of business they do with it. They may not be obliged to withdraw these dividends or patronage refunds but may leave them on deposit to be employed in the society's business operations. The members accumulate collective savings by not distributing the whole surplus but setting aside reserves, creating special funds and depreciating more or less heavily their society's property and equipment. This self-capitalisation, especially when it is carried out on a national scale by federations of Co-operative societies, is a method of generating economic power of the utmost importance. It has been employed, for example, by the consumers' Co-operative Movements of Switzerland and the Scandinavian countries with remarkable results through a further application of the Principle of Association we are now to consider.

On the evidence of their 'Law First', the Rochdale Pioneers intended their Society to follow the pattern set by Dr William

King in *The Co-operator* and grow by a process of intensive development into a self-supporting community providing its members with employment as well as their daily needs. In so far as the Pioneers envisaged collaboration with other societies, it was for the purpose of establishing communities. Yet in the event, when collaboration began on a permanent basis, it was for another purpose with entirely different consequences for the development of the Movement. The practical problem to be solved was the organisation of the wholesale purchasing on behalf of the societies and the avoidance of competition between them in regional wholesale markets at such centres as Manchester. The solution was found by the usual process of trial and error. After experience with a wholesale department, managed by the Pioneers, from which the smaller societies drew supplies, and with the Central Co-operative Agency, which was set up for the societies rather than by them, the leaders of the Rochdale and neighbouring societies concluded that the only true and satisfactory solution lay through a further application of the Principle of Association. They accordingly decided to proceed from the association of individuals to the association of Co-operative societies by constructing, on the basis and with the participation of the primary societies, a Co-operative organisation of the second degree, federal in constitution, which, without infringing the self-government of the societies, should undertake certain common services for them. This organisation, conceived at first as serving the North of England, grew rapidly to national dimensions and, as the Co-operative Wholesale Society Ltd, celebrated its centenary in 1963. It inevitably became the model to be reproduced, with appropriate modifications, by the younger consumers' Co-operative Movements of Europe and other continents.

The further advantages brought by the concentration of the purchasing power of consumers' Co-operative societies in federal wholesale organisations can accordingly be described in general terms applicable to virtually all of them. As in the primary societies, federation makes possible a concentration of capital, at once through the deposit with the wholesale of funds which the societies have no immediate need to employ in their own business and through the retention by the wholesale of a proportion — larger or smaller according to policy — of its trading surpluses, instead of distributing them as dividends on purchases. The combination of purchasing power, backed by an assured market, with capital resources enables the wholesale organisations to gain a foothold, whenever expedient, and often fairly early in their development, in import trade and manufactures, as the CWS did in its first 10 years. They are thus able to embark upon the integration, under the ultimate control and for the sole benefit of the consumers enrolled in their member-societies, of a series of economic operations reaching back towards the sources of raw materials. At each stage of the productive process, given reasonably efficient management, the wholesales are able to retain for their members the equivalent of what would otherwise be the profits of manufacturers and merchants. The advantages of Association in the second degree thus tend to be cumulative.

A notable example of rapid and powerful integrated development is given by one of the best-known regional Co-operative organisations in the USA, the Consumers' Co-operative Association, with headquarters at Kansas City, a main department of whose business is the supply of petroleum products to a membership consisting chiefly of farmers. From the time the tractor began to replace the horse as a source of power, the prices of gasoline and lubricants became an item of growing importance in farmers' costs of production. These prices were manipulated by the petroleum-producing and distributing combines. The farmers accordingly set about reducing them by setting up their own local Co-operative gasoline and service stations. From this beginning in the 1920's, they worked their way, by bulk purchasing through the Consumers' Co-operative Association, to the ownership of cracking plants and refineries and ultimately to their own oilwells and pipelines. Although they did not obtain all the supplies they needed, they did secure an important part of their requirements from their own productive and distributive system, could keep an efficient check on costs and prices, add to their revenues from remunerative by-products and capitalise the profits in order to establish parallel series of enterprises which justified their change of title to Farmland Industries.

The embodiment of the Principle of Association in federal organisations is a pattern of development in fact normal and common to all Co-operative Movements. Just as consumers' societies in retail trade federate in wholesale societies, so credit societies unite in regional or central banks, the primary societies for the collection, storage, and first processing of agricultural produce into marketing federations such as the great Canadian wheat pools or the coffee unions of what was then Tanganyika, and so on. Nor is federation limited to trading, production and finance. All kinds of non-commercial services are provided by associations, under various titles, of Co-operatives. These are mostly national in extent and serve as centres for technical advice, staff training, publicity, the diffusion of Co-operative ideas and information through books and periodicals, the representation before governmental authorities of Co-operative interests and views on public policy, and the maintenance of contact with Co-operative Movements in other lands. They express and conserve whatever sense of unity exists among the Co-operators of the same branch of the Movement in the same country, as well as their feelings of fraternity with Co-operators elsewhere.

The application of the Principle of Association could not stop and, in fact, has not stopped short at national frontiers. Consumers' Co-operative wholesales seeking supplies for their members are driven into world markets, just as are the producers' marketing federations which need direct contact with buyers abroad. Both kinds of organisation sooner or later establish regular trading connections and even depots and offices in other continents than their own. Possibilities of international inter-Co-operative trade were foreseen and discussed at the London International Co-operative Congress of 1895, when the International Co-operative Alliance was founded. Association in the form of permanent organisations of the third degree with a membership drawn from a number of countries was logically indicated. Practically, however, it has been somewhat slow in developing.

The International Co-operative Alliance corresponds in its constitution and functions to the national non-commercial federations mentioned in an earlier paragraph. Throughout its existence it has symbolised the belief of leading Co-operators that their Movement should bring together, in combined efforts to establish a better world economic and social order, men and women of goodwill, irrespective of nationality, race, creed or politics. Despite the interruptions resulting from two world wars, the Alliance has maintained its unity and grown steadily as the Co-operative Movement, in country after country in the different continents, has reached national dimensions and created institutions able to undertake international responsibilities. The Alliance is not restricted in its membership to any particular type of Co-operative enterprise, but accepts as members all which are genuine of their kind.

Apart from the Alliance, it is possible to point to a few other organisations which demonstrate what is not only desirable but possible. The most outstanding is undoubtedly the Scandinavian Co-operative Wholesale Society, Nordisk Andelsforbund. This is the joint purchasing agency set up in the First World War by the wholesale societies of Denmark, Norway and Sweden which were later joined by the two Finnish and the Icelandic wholesale societies. For them it carries on buying operations, mostly outside Europe and especially in tropical countries. Its success prompted the formation in the middle 1950's of a parallel organisation for export trade, Nordisk Andels-Export.

Back in the 1930's the impetus imparted by the growth of the petroleum trade of the Consumers' Co-operative Association led its then director, Howard A. Cowden, to propose the formation of an international Co-operative association to handle fuel oils and lubricants. The Second World War delayed practical operations but the project was revived soon after the war ended, and realised in fact by the formation of the International Co-operative Petroleum Association which continued throughout the 1950's to add to its membership of national Co-operative federations, mostly, though by no means entirely, consumers' Co-operative wholesale societies. In the 1960's it was felt that enough experience and confidence had been gained to justify a policy of expansion and the Association set up in Holland in 1963 what was intended to be the first of a number of processing plants located in various countries. The idea of joint purchase on the international level of farm supplies, notably fertilisers, was first applied about a generation ago by certain of the European agricultural Co-operative wholesale societies, for which the Central Bureau at Rotterdam acted as agent. It is noteworthy that the Central Bureau has in recent years joined the International Co-operative Petroleum Association.

So far the application of the Principle of Association has been discussed mainly by reference to the federation of Co-operative organisations of the same type. These, of course, are much more numerous and conspicuously successful than joint organisations of Co-operatives of different types. Unity to promote common interest is obviously easier to achieve and maintain than unity to promote differing interests, even though they may be mutually complementary. In other words, organisations of producers **or** consumers offer fewer difficulties than organisations of producers **and** consumers. Sometimes the very fact that they are strongly organised separately seems to militate against mutual understanding and joint action between Co-operative producers and consumers. It is worth noting, however, that here and there, even in Europe, where the distinction between the two types of organisation is sharpest, joint institutions have been set up and mutually advantageous trading relations have been established on a permanent basis at local, national and international levels, witness the following examples. In the city of Geneva the retail distribution of milk was carried on for over 30 years by a society in which the local consumers' Co-operative and the Co-operative of dairy farmers who supplied the milk were partners. The arrangement was terminated when the changing structure of retail trade made it necessary for the consumers' society to take sole responsibility for distribution. On the national level, the French consumers' and agricultural Co-operative Movements operate an agreement laying down the general conditions under which inter-trading is carried on between agricultural and consumers' societies. On the international level may be mentioned the organisations created jointly by the English CWS and the Co-operative marketing federations of several Commonwealth countries for the sale of agricultural products, e.g. New Zealand butter, in the United Kingdom, partly though not entirely through the consumers' societies.

The problems of inter-Co-operative relations form part of a series of questions involving applications of the Principle of Unity which are grouped today under the general term of integration. In any national economy the Co-operative sector, if it is at all developed, may be seen to consist of fragmented 'movements' in which the societies and federations serve particular economic interests: the consumers, the farmers, the artisans and so on. If these 'movements' owe a common loyalty and send fraternal delegates to give friendly greetings at one another's congresses, they are not as a rule organically connected and they pursue separate policies determined mainly by the economic interests they severally represent. They may even find themselves on opposing sides in controversies over national economic policy. Hitherto their Co-operative affinities and allegiance to Co-operative Principles have usually been less powerful to bring them together than existing social and economic cleavages to keep them apart. Most of them might well have contentedly drifted along in this fashion, had not radical changes in their economic environment since the Second World War brought a rude awakening.

These changes are too well known to need detailed description here. They can be summarised under two headings: the one, the advent of the welfare state with its concern to promote full employment and rising standards of living among wage and small salary earners; the other, the transformation of distributive trade by new techniques employed by enterprises of unprecedented magnitude. The two are not unconnected, for the chief motive force for the transformation of distribution is the prospect of greater profits from the freer spending of the so-called affluent society. The impact of the new types of enterprise, supermarket chains and so on, brought about a shift, probably irreversible and therefore permanent, in the balance between large-scale and small-scale enterprise in the retail market to the advantage of the former.

For the consumers' Co-operative Movements of all but a few industrially advanced countries, it revealed the two-deck structure described earlier in this chapter — local primary societies plus national federations — to be largely out of date. It showed the Movements, with few exceptions, to be fixed in 19th or early 20th century moulds. The primary societies were still mostly local, small (and therefore too numerous), jealous of their independence and inclined to attempt too much in isolation. Their outlook was parochial and their management efficiency not equal to contemporary requirements. Defective loyalty to the Co-operative wholesales in the matter of purchasing supplies prevented the latter from using the size of the Co-operative market to the fullest advantage. The Movements' lack of cohesion, in short, deprived them of the very advantages of large-scale operation which were being employed against them by their competitors. In every country there were a few alert managers and leaders with foresight who prepared to meet severer competition in good time but the low average level of management skill and wisdom in formulating policy meant that the societies were late in awakening to their situation and slow in reacting to it. It seemed unavoidable that consumers' Co-operation would lose ground, both absolutely and relatively to its large-scale competitors, unless it could accept and carry out with speed a series of structural changes which would permit the consolidation, concentration and centralisation so urgently necessary. It is a sobering thought that many of the measures now regarded as innovations were first put forward by foresighted leaders like J. C. Gray[7] and Ernest Poisson[8] three quarters of a century ago.

The structural changes now required include the fusion of local into regional societies, closer interlocking between them and the federations for the sake of rationalised handling of goods, the transfer of various branches of distribution from local to national management, the organisation of new common services on a national scale, centralised planning and financial control. Their execution is much more than a technical or organisational affair. It requires a change of mental attitude, outlook and sentiment among the Movement's members and leaders. It demands that they have enough faith in their own Principle of Unity, as the ultimate source of the Movement's economic power, to think out anew the forms of association and federation it needs in order to survive and fulfil its proper functions in the contemporary world. Excessive respect for long-standing institutions, old applications of the Principle of Association which have outlived their usefulness, is the chief hindrance to the more comprehensive and dynamic collaboration now demanded of Co-operators, for in many branches of distribution today the true operational unit has ceased to be the local society and can be nothing smaller than the whole national Movement.

Although the preceding paragraphs have been written with special reference to consumers' Co-operative Movements, it has not been forgotten that the enlargement of the scale of economic operations in general, and especially in distribution, has created difficult problems for agricultural Co-operation also. The big distributor, like the supermarket chain, is skilful and ruthless in exerting power on the producer, particularly the small man. The expansion of the so-called broiler industry, which supplies the large provision dealers with poultry prepared for the table, has been accompanied by the spread of contract farming, a system under which the big concern offers the farmer an assured market and cash return, provided that he will undertake to supply chickens bred, fed and prepared for the market as the big distributor requires them.

Agricultural Co-operative organisations rightly regard this as a most insidious attack on the farmers' independence which it has always been one of their chief functions to safeguard. Their own authority, however, and their command over the loyalty of their members are likely to be undermined, unless they can offer them benefits comparable with those held out by contract farming. In this situation the agricultural Co-operative organisations rightly seek to ally themselves with the consumers' organisations with a large supermarket trade as their natural partners in building up an inter-Co-operative marketing system which provides an alternative to the subordination of the producer (or the consumer) to large-scale profit enterprises. Such integration within the Co-operative sector is, of course, one of the most difficult forms in which the Principle of Association needs to be applied in the contemporary world. It demands a realisation of the mutuality of interest of consumer and producer which may be called the *pons asinorum* of Co-operative theory and practice. Yet the harder the pressure grows on the Co-operative sector from the governmental and capitalist sectors, the more will the different branches of Co-operation be obliged to study and support one another and the less will it be practically possible for them to advance independently in their respective ruts.

A special case of the problem of welding Co-operative consumers' and producers' organisations together in a common, coherent system is presented by the growth of Co-operation in the developing regions and clamant needs of the latter to market their products in the economically advanced countries. To expect the newly-liberated nations to make progress without enabling them to obtain a steadily increasing share of world trade is to ask them to lift themselves by their own boot-strings. The young Co-operatives of those countries expect more than good advice and technical assistance from the older Movements; they want exchanges of goods and services on an equal business footing. But between the consumers' Co-operative Movements in the temperate zones, working their way back to the sources of raw materials, and the Co-operative Movements of tropical producers of raw materials, working their way forward to their ultimate export markets, there exist, for example in the soap and edible oil industries, mammoth capitalist combines competing with each in its own sphere and only likely to be circumvented, to say nothing of dislodged, by the interlocking of the two forms of Co-operation and co-ordinated action at both ends of the productive process.

No less important, and even vitally so in the early stages of their development, are the relations of Co-operative Movements with their national governments and the need for mutual support through their own federations to replace as soon as possible tutelage by government departments. The second half of the 20th century has seen a remarkable increase in the variety of forms Co-operative Association may take and the range of economic interests which may have recourse to it, not least the countries where more or less 'affluent' economies have unexpectedly declined into a state of depression for which scarcely any other palliative than Co-operation can be found. The lack of contact between these new Co-operatives and the older Co-operative Movement, as well as the absence of cohesion with one another, reduces the term 'Co-operative sector' to a merely arithmetical or statistical expression. This lack of a common organ for reciprocal contact and consultation for the representation of the Co-operative Movement as a whole in its dealings with government (and other external organisations) is the most obvious structural weakness of many, if not most national Co-operative Movements. To overcome it, French Co-operatives succeeded by persistent persuasion over a number of years in bringing every branch of their Movement into a single representative association, the Groupement National de la Coopération, one of its functions being to express their united views to government on any appropriate subject. When a Co-operative and governmental view coincide, the Groupement becomes the instrument of efficient and fruitful collaboration. It is also the medium for harmonious collaboration between the Co-operative organisations themselves and the mutual benefit societies which observe the same principles as the Co-operatives. Together they form the bulk of the social sector of the economy which the government recognises as being separate and essentially different from private and State enterprise.

The track followed by the preceding discussion of the Principle of Association or Unity has led from the constitution of primary and secondary Co-operative organisations 100 years or more ago to contemporary problems of world economy. That is not surprising, for it is through successively widening applications of this Principle that the Co-operative Movement has grown to world dimensions. The only real limits to its application are world limits. Artificial limits, of course, are imposed or accepted, often unconsciously, by Co-operators on their own thinking or creative planning. One of the commonest of these is to conceive unity as being essentially static and to forget its dynamic aspects and uses. Granted that unity is essential to the stability of Co-operative institutions, the power which springs from it can and must be expressed in mobility and flexibility no less than in rigidity. After all a Movement must, by definition, move, that is, change. In our generation the Movement's worst internal obstacles to its progress and development are found in excessive reverence for traditional institutions and usages, allied with too much consideration for minority vested interests which cluster around them. The narrower unity is allowed to block the road to the broader. To change the simile, just as crustaceans grow by shedding their shells, so the developing Co-operative Movement has to burst its way out of cramping institutions it has outgrown and clothe itself in new ones in which it can freely grapple with new and greater tasks. To be able to make this transition, not merely smoothly and rapidly, but at all, many more Co-operators, and especially those exercising leadership, must be able to keep clearly and steadily in mind the underlying unity of all the specialised forms of Co-operation. The fact that the Co-operative Movement has attained world-wide extension means that its future development must lie more and more along lines of closer and stronger integration of its multitudinous fragments.

CHAPTER THREE

Economy

The power which Co-operators derive from Association is exercised mainly in the economic field and for economic ends. Economic advantage is the motive which attracts to the Co-operative Movement the great majority of its adherents and its economic performance sets the standard by which they judge its value to them. Unless their membership of a Co-operative society enables them to effect savings which they would not otherwise be able to make or yields them an income in money or provides a service which they would not otherwise receive, there is scarcely any advantage in their being Co-operators, whatever moral or social benefits Co-operation may offer. Usually there must be very compelling economic reasons for the majority of people to take the trouble to form, join or run Co-operative societies at all. In this sense it is true (although not the whole truth) that Co-operation is the offspring of poverty and distress.

Co-operative organisations and their operations must therefore inevitably be subject to what may be called the economic test. This takes the form of a double comparison which may be expressed in a twofold question: does Co-operation provide the same benefits for less cost than other systems or does it provide greater benefits for an equal cost? The comparison of Co-operation with alternative systems, that is, ordinary profit enterprise or government-organised services, is thus made in respect of another comparison, that is, between benefits and costs. Nature offers man very little for nothing. Certainly there is no economic growth or social progress, even in the most favourable of climates, without labour and thought. The measurement of results against efforts and sacrifices required to obtain them is a very far-reaching principle in human life and extends beyond the sphere commonly called economic. We speak by analogy of the economy of means by which an artist or poet achieves his effects. By a further analogy, Co-operation, as an art of association, yields its material and social advantages only to those who meet its demands for effort, sacrifice and self-discipline.

The essence of Co-operative Economy is the assumption by an association of the functions of ownership, organisation and risk-bearing usually discharged by an individual, partnership or company of entrepreneurs. This runs counter in several ways to the system of specialisation on which modern economic development is based. In particular, it implies that groups of people, lacking specialised training or experience, can enter into commerce, industry, banking or insurance and hold their chosen ground alongside enterprises directed and managed by business people with years of technical training. Thus consumers set up retail stores, industrial wage-earners their own factories, farmers their own warehouses and processing plants, would-be borrowers their own banks, tenants their own housing societies and so on. To adapt the words of Dr Samuel Johnson,[1] the wonder is not that they do it well, but that they do it at all. Obviously, although the functions of the entrepreneur are assumed by a society, some are in fact exercised in Co-operatives of any size by delegation and are delegated to an increasing degree as Co-operative undertakings grow in magnitude and complexity. Even so, this does not dispose of the extraordinary, even astonishing, fact that, in the final analysis, the specialist manager or director or administrator is accountable to the lay-membership, subject to its authority and bound by its decisions.

We accordingly return to the reasons, alluded to in an earlier paragraph, for which producers and consumers associate in order to play an unaccustomed role as entrepreneurs. Modern economic life is permeated by division of labour and the exchange of goods and services through markets. Historically, Co-operation originated in the market economy. The Co-operative idea was discovered, applied and propagated 100 to 150 years ago by people who found themselves unfavourably placed, either as buyers or as sellers, in the market economy. These are, notably, the ultimate consumers and the producers of primary products. Today the most widely extended and powerful Co-operative Movements are precisely those engaged in the related fields of marketing and distribution, i.e. the consumers' and agricultural Co-operative Movements. But the other branches of Co-operation are also, to a greater or lesser degree, concerned with markets of particular kinds, e.g. for land, houses and dwellings; for services, such as electric power or medical care.

Applying the Principle of Association, those who find themselves in a situation of permanent disadvantage in the market buy their requirements or sell their products collectively in order to bring about a fall or rise in prices in their favour. The object of the associated consumers (or other buyers) is in the long run to obtain their requirements at prices which represent real costs, not inflated prices. The object of the associated producers likewise is to obtain for their products prices which correspond to their full market value and yield them a reasonable livelihood. The widening price-spread today between what the final consumers pay and what the farmers receive for many food products indicates that those aims are by no means necessarily inconsistent with each other. The determining factors which impelled action in either case were originally — and still are today in all the newly-developing regions — not so much beckoning advantages as driving forces: hunger, squalor, exploitation and deprivation, coupled with the conviction that none of these evils is really necessary or irremediable.

Co-operators have never been happy about the virtues of the market economy, as a mechanism for exchange, ascribed to it by classical economists. Their experience teaches them otherwise. They regard the market mechanism as no more than a rough and ready and, at times, highly unreliable indicator of society's real needs. This is a serious fault in an economic system in which production must necessarily be undertaken in anticipation and on estimates of future demand. The demand to which the market responds is, in any case, not social need but the demand which is called by economists 'effective' because backed by ability to pay. Moreover, market price is falsified as an indicator when it results from excessive differences in bargaining power or position between buyers on the one hand and sellers on the other, so that one is able to exploit the relative weakness of the other. Every housewife who has had to pay rising prices when war is threatened and shortages are anticipated, or the fisherman and farmer who are faced with marketing a superabundant catch or crop, understand this very well. But, special crises apart, the play of the market can keep certain classes of consumers and producers in a position of permanent inferiority in bargaining power, so long at any rate as they do not find a remedy in Co-operation. Finally, it is notorious that market price is continually subject to attempts, more or less successful, to manipulate or regulate it, particularly through the control of prices, limitation of supplies and the division of markets by larger or smaller combinations of enterprises (cartels or trusts) which may suppress mutual competition to the point of oligopoly or monopoly. The constant abuse of bargaining power sooner or later provokes, as the American economist Galbraith has described, the emergence of countervailing forces tending to restore equilibrium and among these Co-operative organisations can often be included.

Successful Co-operative organisation tends, other things being equal, to strengthen the position and increase the bargaining or competitive power of its participants in a given market, sometimes to the extent of permitting them effectively to influence or even regulate prices. It can also enable them to by-pass a market through the integration of successive stages of production or distribution under unified direction, as in many of the consumers' wholesales or farmers' supply federations. But it should and often does go further than this. The fact that, in a Co-operative society, a group of people requiring economic services for their own purpose, be that housekeeping or running a farm or workshop, replaces the ordinary entrepreneur trading for profit, allows play to a different set of aims and motives, besides resulting in different business policies. Without endorsing all that Charles Gide wrote in a celebrated passage in praise of the reconciliation of conflicting economic interests effected by Co-operative organisations, it may be observed that in a consumers' Co-operative society the old battle of wits between housewife and retailer no longer has any meaning. This different concept of Economy underlies certain practices of the Rochdale Pioneers which were radical departures from the trading methods of their day. Take, for example, the rule laying down that the Society should distribute pure goods and deliver just weight. To do anything else would be, from the consumers' standpoint, false economy, nor is there any need for either the legal rule of *caveat emptor* or for government inspection backed by penalties to deter the retailer from profiteering at the expense of the consumers' ignorance or lack of acumen. The Principle of Economy, applied through Co-operation, enables the consumers' or users' interests in the value of commodities in use to play an important, sometimes dominating role. Housing Co-operatives offer brilliant illustrations of the same tendency. If they came into existence primarily to check rent exploitation under modern urban conditions, they have developed by setting new and higher standards of dwelling accommodation and ancillary services, not for their own members alone, but for the community at large. It is no accident, but a natural consequence of the Co-operative concept of Economy, that housing Co-operatives construct the best low-cost dwellings in Europe and, perhaps, in the United States also.

Again, to add an example from agriculture, one of the greatest benefits conferred by Co-operation on farmers anywhere is the control it gives them over the quality of farm requirements, with the assurance that they get what they pay for in seeds that germinate, fertilisers that enrich the soil and fodder that nourishes their livestock. This interest in the quality of products is not confined to the Co-operatively organised consumers or buyers. Again and again, Co-operative marketing provides direct incentives to producers to seek higher returns through improved qualities. The evolution and results of the Co-operative marketing of butter, bacon and eggs in Denmark furnish classic examples which bring students and inquirers from all over the world and need no description here. A simple example from the very beginning of Co-operative promotion in China may be, however, of interest. In the 1930's when Dr J. B. Tayler[2] was encouraging Co-operative marketing among the farmers in the region of Tientsin, he had hard work to persuade them not to try to cheat the merchants by adding stones and gravel when baling their cotton for sale. They reluctantly consented to send clean bales as an experiment, but the higher prices the merchants paid when they knew the weights were not falsified finally convinced them. The appearance in recent years of non-trading consumers' associations testing various types of commodity and deciding which of a number of competing products is the 'best buy' gives evidence that the idea of value for money is by no means dead or dormant in our contemporary 'affluent' society.

This may be the appropriate moment to examine in the light of the Principle of Economy the Rochdale Rule of cash payments, the observance of which under present day conditions has been sharply challenged, and indeed abandoned, in certain important branches of Co-operative retailing in some countries during the last generation. With every respect for the 1930–1937 ICA Committee Report, the system of cash payments is not a Principle in itself, but it is one of the most effective applications which the Rochdale Pioneers gave to the Principle of Economy. They recognised that it was the simplest, safest and cheapest system for both the Co-operative and the member. For the society, it simplifies accounting, tends to keep costs down, minimises risks, avoids the accumulation of bad and doubtful debts and helps to conserve capital for development. For the member, it exerts a healthy influence on the domestic budget by reducing or avoiding temptations to overspend and by reinforcing habits of thrift. Credit trading by consumers' retail societies seems fundamentally inconsistent with Co-operative ideas of Economy. That does not mean there is no place in contemporary Co-operative economics for consumer credit. There is, if only to enable wage-earners to enjoy the rapid rise in their standards of comfort that technical progress continually makes possible. There is also an appropriate form of Co-operation — the credit union — to provide it. It is, however, the mixture of retailing with what is essentially banking that is unsound from the standpoint of the Principle of Economy, because it prevents the real efficiency of Co-operative merchandising from being clearly seen and judged.

It can be speciously argued, of course, that to grant credit is necessary in order to attract and not repel custom; that credit trading by increasing turnover tends to reduce the cost ratio; and that, as in any case it is the prevailing custom of the trade in dry goods and consumer durables, the Co-operative Movement must concede to it or lose ground. This line of argument is unacceptable for several reasons. If the Rochdale Pioneers had been content to copy their competitors they would never have made a success, not of cash trading alone, but of their Society's business. Nor would they have helped a single household to liberate itself from debt. So far from doing as their competitors do, consumers' Co-operatives should constantly aim at offering consumers something demonstrably better. Even in the field of credit itself, consumers' Co-operatives could and should, by correlation with credit unions as in the United States, offer their members credit at rates of interest almost ridiculously low compared with those in ordinary instalment or hire-purchase transactions. Above all, they should abstain from competitive pressure on their members to contract credit obligations to such an extent that they have too little income left, after meeting their periodic repayments, to pay on the nail when a suitable chance occurs to buy something for cash.

There is probably little room for disagreement about the unsoundness of unregulated open credit, on the one hand, or the legitimacy of credit, repayable in instalments, for the large consumer durables such as furniture, kitchen equipment and television sets, on the other. What is more open to dispute is the provision of credit in the intermediate field of current expenditure on dry-goods, particularly drapery, clothing, household utensils and so on.

What is decisive in this connection is how much the standard of living of the working classes has risen since the days of the Rochdale Pioneers. For them, as for their original members, cash payments were an indispensable safety measure. It may well be so today in some of the less developed countries. Where Co-operative storekeeping is still in its pioneer stage and Co-operative education at a low standard, it would be advantageous to operate a strict cash payments system to diminish the risk of failure.

This would be all the easier if credit unions were available. Co-operative credit unions are spreading all over the world and can be organised alongside consumers' stores. They have the great advantage of encouraging saving by their membership as well as imposing a discipline on their loan business. Thoughtless or reckless borrowing is restrained because the purpose of every loan has to be approved by the authorities of the union before the member can draw any cash. A desirable separation of trading from banking functions could also be achieved in countries of advanced economic development by the introduction of a credit union system.

A similar result can be obtained in countries like Great Britain where the consumer Co-operatives are supported by a Co-operative Bank of national dimensions. In some British societies there is an arrangement whereby, if a member buys on credit, it is the Co-operative Bank and not the Co-operative society which finances the debt and receives the repayment. The society is thus able to economise its capital (for which it should have a dozen better uses than lending to members) and the system ought to become the general rule throughout the country.

The argument that the consumers' Co-operative must conform to credit-trading competitors fails entirely to account for the striking success of firms doing an enormous and expanding trade for cash in, for example, ready-made clothes, with precisely the public for which the consumers' societies should cater and whose support it should have attracted and held from the beginning. Too many concessions to credit trading, coupled with the absence of a satisfactory Co-operative alternative, signify not the need to revise Rochdale Principles but rather what Fourier once called 'a lack of genius' on the part of contemporary Co-operators.

In the period of relative tranquillity before the First World War, the British and certain European consumers' Co-operative Movements differed notably in the respective ways in which they displayed their economic advantages. Whereas the British were inclined to pursue a policy of high dividends on purchases even if this entailed charging higher than market prices, the Continentals tended to charge lower than market prices, even if this meant lower dividends on purchases. In the disturbed conditions which prevailed after the Second World War, purchasing power shrank, prices rose, profit margins narrowed and dividends dwindled. The cost of keeping record of members' purchases became increasingly burdensome.

With the return of more settled conditions, the distributive revolution brought new forms of competition, together with higher wages and salaries and greater spending power. Lower dividends were less powerful attractions to customers. When for a time it was the fashion among retailers to give trading stamps to their customers with the goods they bought, a number of Co-operatives joined in and worked their own forms of stamp scheme. The stamps were saved by the customer (or member) who, having saved a given quantity, could tender them for goods, obtain cash or have the value credited to his or her share account. This system was given a Co-operative gloss by being called 'dividend' stamps but all that it had to do with dividend was that it replaced it. The original and only genuine dividend was a share of a surplus or profit, if one was made in an accounting period, but the stamps were given before it was known whether there would be a surplus or not. It was, in short, a bribe and a cost.

The disappearance or diminished importance of the dividend on purchases has led some societies in Great Britain to seek other means of emphasising the difference between their members and those purchasers who are simply customers. Various schemes such as special offers and discounts, the benefit of which is reserved exclusively for members, have been introduced. In Switzerland for many years past, consumer Co-operatives have countered the competition of private traders in the form of rebates or discounts by offering members the choice of an immediate discount at the time of purchase or waiting for the dividend at the end of the business year. In Germany, the Dortmund Society books a whole theatre or opera house for a performance reserved exclusively for its members. In Canada a number of Co-operatives work on the 'direct charge' system which enables them to undersell their competitors. Yet there is still something to be said for a dividend system, if there is a surplus, as evidence of a Co-operative's superiority. Surely in these days of computers it should be possible to restore a genuine dividend system based on a cheap method of recording members' purchases. Social dividends have also been advocated as substitutes for cash dividends and correspond to some of the ways in which the ICA Commission indicated that surplus can be employed consistently with Principle. At the wholesale level Sweden and Switzerland notably do without dividends to member societies and capitalise all surpluses for purposes of development.

Returning from that digression we take up again the point made in an earlier paragraph that the Co-operative system permits other motives than profit and gain through investment to play an essential role in economic organisation. This is to be seen not only in the trading practice of Co-operative societies, but also in the processes by which Co-operative Movements develop. Since the primary objective of Co-operatives of all kinds is to promote the economy of their members, their effectiveness and efficiency are judged by the services and other benefits rendered to their members, not simply by their profitability as enterprises. Similar considerations govern the expansion of Co-operative Movements both horizontally and vertically. In most consumers' Co-operative Movements, for example, may be seen emerging a kind of normal order or scheme of priorities according to which new services are initiated, based on the relative urgency of various wants. Most consumers' Co-operatives begin by distributing food or, if not, food soon becomes their most important line of business. Food is a primary want and, among foods, bread (or rice) may take priority over all other foodstuffs when members' incomes are too low to allow a very liberal diet. Bread, groceries and provisions, meat, milk, vegetables and fruit, cleaning materials and other daily household requisites, including oil and hard fuel; footwear and clothing; drapery and furniture — this is generally the order of priority which is, of course, not absolute but liable to slight variations according to circumstances, technical difficulties to be overcome and the financial resources available.

This scheme of development is reflected in the relative importance of the distributive turnover or productive output of the different categories of goods, as well as in the time-order in which ventures into new fields are made. The overwhelming importance hitherto of foodstuffs in the business volume of consumers' Co-operative Movements, almost without exception, is thus accounted for. A modifying factor may be seen operating in Sweden and some other countries where the policy of the consumer Co-operative Movement has been influenced by the Swedish example. In these countries, entry into production and to some extent distribution may be conditioned by opportunities of rendering service, not to the Co-operative membership alone but to the whole community of consumers, by breaking into a market controlled by a cartel or ring of suppliers and bringing about through effective competition (lower prices, a superior product or both together) a considerable fall in prices. The determining factor is whether scope is given for competition by the excessive prices the cartel forces the public to pay for the article or services supplied.

The interaction between member and society which is fundamental in Co-operative economic organisation gives rise to another noteworthy feature to which Albert Thomas,[3] first Director of the International Labour Office, called attention in a passage of his report to the International Labour Conference of 1932. He wrote: 'The structure of the Co-operative economic system, based as it is on a very large number of small economic units which are like antennae through which it can sense the requirements and possibilities of everyday life, has a sort of sensory apparatus comparable to that of a living body. That apparatus does not simply transmit information step by step to the central organs which translate it in to reasoned actions. It even, up to a certain point, permits automatic reactions, defensive or compensatory reflexes, which prevent maladjustment and avoid dangerous error. Thus, for example, the centralisation of statistics, often on the basis of standardised book-keeping, provides the great Co-operative federations with detailed information and comprehensive surveys; and they can thus learn lessons of which they can at once take advantage in order to correct their methods, remedy omissions, prevent wastage, get rid of unnecessary machinery, avoid maladjustment in management and reduce excessive overhead charges'.

The sensory apparatus described by Albert Thomas works, of course, in two directions. The experience of Co-operative organisations of the markets in which they operate is conveyed back to their members and enlightens them in the conduct of their own economic affairs. The most conspicuous examples come very probably from the agricultural Co-operative Movements, many of which not only transmit to their farmer-members new ideas on the handling of stock or crops, but give cogent reasons for adopting them and provide the material or financial means of carrying them out. Only too often, and much more so before the rise of agricultural Co-operation, the typical farmer knows little or nothing about the market for which his produce is ultimately destined. It is screened from his view by the host of middlemen to whom he directly sells, none of whom has any interest in enlightening him.

What Co-operation taught the Danish farmer about the British market, to which his butter, bacon and eggs began to be exported in the last quarter of the 19th century, made him ready to accept and carry out revolutionary changes in cropping and treating livestock, including the breeding of an entirely new type of pig which yielded bacon conforming to British taste. Similar enlightenment is being spread today wherever Co-operative marketing is successful — in Africa among the growers of coffee, cocoa and palm oil, in Asia and Oceania among copra producers — but not only in agriculture; in artisanal industry closer contact with the market is weaning craftsmen away from traditional products and designs to experiment with new things more attractive to the present-day buyer. It is worthy of note that Co-operation thereby benefits consumers as well as the producers for whom it may have been primarily intended.

The purpose of Albert Thomas in the passage already quoted was to point out that the Co-operative Movement is by nature disposed to economic planning. He wrote his report at the depth of the depression in the 1930's when there was widespread concern to find palliatives or remedies for the alternate booms and slumps of the market economy and the continual lack of equilibrium between demand and supply, needs and purchasing power, saving and investment, which resulted in bankruptcy, insecurity and unemployment for millions. Laisser faire as a policy was assumed to be dead. The ideas of John Maynard Keynes[4] reinforced the inclination towards 'managed' economies. Governments were more and more expected, not only to rescue the casualties of economic depression but also to find means of forestalling or averting these crises. In contrast to the economic chaos of the West there stood out the regulated economy of the USSR in which development was promoted and the national product apportioned under the control of a central planning authority. Albert Thomas's thesis was that, in the Co-operative Movement, reasoned organisation replaced the so-called 'laws' of an individualistic economy of which private profit supplied the motive power, and that its basic principles demanded a policy of systematic planning. He wanted the member-governments of the International Labour Organisation to study the constitution and working methods of the Co-operative Movement in order to learn how a planned economy could take account of fundamental economic needs.

The member-governments might have learned more had the Co-operative Movement been full value in practice for the bold claims Albert Thomas put forward. But even if what he asserted related more to the Movement's potential than to its actual performance, examples enough can be produced to show that Co-operation is an influence making for order and discipline, in contrast to the Gadarene rushes after profit and flights away from losses characteristic of the unregulated market economy. In short, Co-operation implies planning and the consistent application of its Principle of Economy tends towards planning on a steadily increasing scale. Taking first the demand side of the market, we may note the consumers' Co-operative whose members accept to a greater or lesser extent the self-discipline demanded by loyal and consistent purchasing from its stores and cease to purchase indiscriminately in all kinds of shops. By doing so they permit their society to estimate and forecast their recurrent requirements of different commodities more narrowly than is possible for a business with a fluctuating clientele.

The society tends to constitute an organised market the demands of which are known. By so doing it fulfils an essential requirement of a modern economy — an assured rather than a speculative guide to production. Because of the federal structure described in Chapter Two the same advantages are enjoyed by the wholesales which purchase and manufacture for the consumers' societies. Their accumulating data enables them to establish statistically normal rates of expansion, learn how to estimate future needs with accuracy and lay their plans for new trading departments and factories accordingly. In another sphere, the societies can acquire, through the exchange of experience, a stock of ideas and practical rules which they can apply almost automatically to given situations. These account for the reflex actions mentioned by Albert Thomas. Discipline is reinforced by the auditing powers exercised in many countries by Co-operative unions. What has been aptly called 'union discipline' has been built up by generations of painstaking supervision and staff training.

Passing over to the supply side of the market, we may again note that order and discipline are prerequisites and also results of successful agricultural Co-operation. Producer Co-operators accept a parallel of self-discipline to that of consumer Co-operators when they cease to do their own selling and hand over the disposal of their produce to a Co-operative. It is commonly the practice to reinforce this self-discipline by requiring the producer-members formally to contract to supply to the Co-operative for processing and sale the whole of their output of a given commodity, except the small quantity retained for their own use at home or on the farm.

This is the well-known 'binding rule' which gives the Co-operative command of bulk, maximises its bargaining power and enables it to secure additional advantages under the general head of orderly marketing. First, the commodity may be standardised, uniformity of quality being attained by such means as payments to members of a dairy society on the basis of the fat-content of the milk they supply for butter-making. Second, where uniformity is out of the question, the society often grades its members' produce, thus enabling higher prices to be received for better qualities instead of a low price for an undifferentiated consignment. Third, there is the regulation of supplies to the market. If the Co-operative has adequate warehouse accommodation, the farmers, instead of rushing to market their crops as soon as harvested and so depressing prices against their own interest, deliver them to their Co-operative which stores and, if necessary, processes them, releasing them to the market by instalments spread over the whole crop-year. Prices are steadied thereby, the fall at the beginning and the rise at the end of each crop-year, as supplies grow short, being minimised. The producer-member is paid, of course, a reasonable advance on delivery of his crop and sometimes receives interim payments and a final instalment when the trading results for the whole crop-year are known. If there is an unsold surplus the society or the federation to which it is affiliated would normally carry that forward into the following year or longer and it may often help to even out supplies if years of deficient harvests follow years of abundance. The classic examples are, of course, the operations of the famous grain-growers' elevator societies and their federations — the pools — which handle and market the greater part of Canada's wheat production.

Nor did Albert Thomas fail to point out that such orderly marketing could be, and is, carried forward into the field of inter-Co-operative trade. 'The planning system on which Co-operative activity is organised,' he told the International Labour Conference, 'is extended and completed by the endeavours which are made to link up consumers'

Co-operative societies and agricultural selling Co-operative societies in a more or less organised whole, thus ensuring that the former receive a uniform and regular supply of goods and that the latter can count on a steady market, the requirements of which can be foreseen.' This thesis was reaffirmed 11 years later by a resolution of the Hot Springs Conference which was the precursor of the present Food and Agriculture Organisation of the United Nations.

Efforts to integrate the orderly marketing of the agricultural Co-operative Movement with the orderly distribution of the consumers' Co-operative Movement are constantly being made and will continue to be made, for the obvious reason that no more economical method of handling farm produce on its journey from the land to the larder has yet been devised. Admittedly, the practical and psychological difficulties in the way of its realisation are stubborn and sometimes baffling. Yet the idea is not Utopian. In respect, for example, of Danish butter it was realised for a long time. In addition Co-operative supplies of pork products, sausages, delicatessen items and canned goods from Denmark are imported into Britain by the Co-operative Wholesale Society and subsequently retailed by its affiliated consumers' societies.

A similar pattern can and must, with time and purposeful effort, be worked out for a number of other food products now being handled by producers' as well as consumers' Co-operative organisations, although their operations still wait to be co-ordinated in unbroken chains of Co-operatively controlled processes. Parallel to these chains and complementary to them, others must be constructed in order to bring the Co-operative products of the highly industrialised countries within the reach of Co-operators of regions beginning their modern economic development.

These are the objectives towards which the economic planning of the Co-operative Movement necessarily leads. Their attainment depends on the growth of the Movement's economic power, first through the increasing magnitude and strength of its several branches and, second, through their closer and more effective integration. The pace of the advance can be quickened by the general adoption and enforcement by the directorates of all Co-operative trading organisations of a simple policy rule, namely that given equality of prices and conditions, a Co-operative market or source of supply shall invariably be preferred. But above all, those practical operations need to be guided and inspired by a concept of Co-operation as a whole derived from the Principle of Unity considered in a previous chapter. With its aid Co-operators may yet come within sight of the consummation of the application of their Principle of Economy, namely the international organisation of exchange to which trade is no more than the first step.

Co-operative economic organisation needs time in which to implant itself and reveal all its inherent virtues. The Movement is thus exposed in more than one way to the risk of frustration. Its dynamic power may decline through losing the vision of its ultimate aims and ideals. Its short-term or adventitious economic benefits, which are by-products, may be mistaken for its true long-term objectives. The exaggerated importance frequently attached to its dividend (patronage refund) system and the debasement of this system into a custom-catching device is a notable example of this danger. But time also reveals an even greater danger in the tendency, pointed out again and again by George Russell, the great Irish Co-operator, for the antagonists in any struggle to acquire each other's characteristics. If Co-operative Movements have achieved success in imposing some of their own standards on ordinary trade, they have themselves often become commercialised in spirit. Co-operation may become assimilated to the profit economy and so lose its power to reform or correct a system which can (and often does) achieve its purpose by producing not only wealth, but what John Ruskin called 'illth'.

Naturally, the full economic value of Co-operative Principles only becomes evident in so far as Co-operatives are technically on an equal footing with profit enterprise. Yet to seek or achieve technical parity is not of itself enough. If Co-operation is to conserve its dynamic power or recover it when temporarily lost, the Movement must go back for inspiration to its first Principles and reinterpret them in a manner apposite to human society in its present situation.

For it is only through Association that men and women can master the spirit of lucre and relegate it to its proper place in human affairs.

Though wealth in the narrower, material sense of the term and the power it gives are objectives of Co-operative Economy, it is not because of any value the Movement may attach to them as ends in themselves, but because their proper use promotes higher standards of human life to which Co-operation's other Principles also contribute. The economic test is not the only one which Co-operation has to pass. It will be ultimately judged by its contributions to the achievement of satisfaction and security for the exploited, deprived and depressed peoples of the world.

CHAPTER FOUR

Democracy

The differences between Co-operation and other economic systems, revealed in the course of discussing its Principles of Association and Economy, become more clearly discernible as we consider its Principle of Democracy. These differences have led more than a few Co-operators to regard Democracy as the most vital of all the Principles. Reasons for not accepting this view and for taking Association as the true fundamental were suggested in the chapter dealing with that Principle. Nevertheless, it may be conceded that Democracy is the logical *differentia* or the major feature which distinguishes Co-operation as a system of economic organisation. Despite the fact that Robert Owen's community experiments were conducted on paternalistic rather than democratic lines, it is hardly possible to conceive of Co-operative societies existing or working under any other than a democratic system of government. The British working men who launched the first Co-operative Movement under the inspiration of Robert Owen and Dr William King were therefore right to follow their instincts and endow their societies with democratic constitutions.

After all, a Co-operative exists to promote the interests of the whole body of its membership. It must be managed with the consent and approval of the members, otherwise it will collapse. There must therefore be agreed methods of ascertaining the members' wishes, as well as safeguards against the society being managed or manipulated in the interests of a minority of them or of a single dominating individual or, yet again, of some external power, authority or institution. The simplest solution to these problems is to give all members equal voting power and to make the management responsible exclusively to them. The ICA Committee of 50 years ago adopted the formula 'Democratic control — one member, one vote'. In practice, however, and especially in the large and complex Co-operative organisations of today, much more is needed than the rule of 'one member, one vote' to ensure the reality of democratic administration. Indeed rules, although indispensable, are not by themselves sufficient to maintain the democratic character of a Co-operative society, as it is hoped to make clear in the subsequent discussion.

Abraham Lincoln's description of democracy as government of the people by the people for the people expresses the essence of political democracy, but is too simple for direct application to associations whose objects and functions are primarily economic. It is not the members of a Co-operative society who have to be governed but their common affairs which have to be administered. The society's power to promote their economic interests has to be used wisely and effectively for their advantage as they conceive it. This necessarily involves technical processes which cannot be operated by any and every member. The simplest of village credit societies needs a secretary-treasurer. An ordinary members' meeting can hardly be conducted without a chairman. In short, there are inevitably operations which must be entrusted to committees or individual officers, to whom is delegated the authority which resides in the membership as a whole. The present discussion of Democracy in Co-operative organisations therefore requires an examination of the powers reserved and exercised by the members as a body, the powers exercised by elected or appointed officers, the institutions through which these powers are channelled and their mutual relations and reactions. Because the Co-operative Movement is in continual evolution, this examination must be concerned not simply with the statics or stability of Co-operative organisations but with their dynamics also.

The basis of a democratic system in a Co-operative or other association is constituted by the means or machinery for ascertaining and expressing the general will of the members. By general will is meant, of course, not the sum of all their individual wills which, by cancelling one another out, may easily amount to nothing, but their will when they are seeking their common good as members of their society and considering its affairs from that standpoint. Corresponding to Abraham Lincoln's idea of government **by** the people, the role of the members in a Co-operative must be active rather than passive. There is certain guidance they alone can give, certain decisions they alone can take. If these are not forthcoming, or if they are unenlightened or in other ways falsified, the democratic process fails to work. In order that the members shall discharge their role effectively, two rights have to be assured under the rules of their society: the right to be informed and the right to be consulted. In the rules and practices of the Rochdale Pioneers Society these rights were secured by the convocation of regular and frequent meetings for the consideration of the Society's business and by the presentation of periodic reports and duly audited balance sheets for questions, discussion and eventual adoption.

Normally, the organ through which the general will is expressed is the general meeting which all members have the right to attend and in which each has one vote and no one more than one. The special cases of federations and of large societies governed by a representative assembly will be considered later. In primary societies with simple constitutions — and these are the great majority all over the world — the members duly convened in general meeting are sovereign in the society. For that reason the convocation of general meetings is usually subject to precise rules and their procedure often governed by standing orders. At the very beginning of a society's existence the members have to adopt its rules before they can be applied or enforced and to elect representatives to serve as a management committee and probably other officers. With the passage of time they are inevitably called upon to renew the mandates of these officers or replace them by others, to adopt amendments of a rule which may have become necessary or desirable and to review the business operations of the society, with the right to express their satisfaction or dissatisfaction with the management. If decisions are required, a majority vote decides, failing unanimity. If majorities do not always truly or fully express the general will, it is possible that minorities will express it even less accurately. In any case minorities which believe they are right have opportunities of converting the majority to their view which, if they are successful, then becomes the general will. As an additional safeguard against decisions out of harmony with the general will, it is usually provided in the rules of societies that on certain vital matters, e.g. the amendment of the rules, dissolution or merger, resolutions can be adopted only if they are carried by a majority of not less than two-thirds of the members present and voting in general meetings specially convened for the purpose.

The effectiveness of the general meeting as a democratic organ depends not so much on its function, as defined by the rules, as on the proportion of the membership it attracts and the standard of knowledge, common sense and community sense reached in its discussions. These in turn very often depend upon and may be adversely affected by accidental factors like the availability or location of meeting places, especially if a society has no hall of its own. Halls, as an investment of capital which entails expense and seldom brings a net revenue, are apt to be regarded with jealousy by the heads of trading departments with use for the space. On the other hand, the Waltham Land-purchase and Housing Society, near Kingston in Jamaica, which made a meeting place for its members by laying a concrete floor under a shed outside its office, displayed admirable democratic wisdom. The greatest threats to the effectiveness of the general meeting in the long run, however, usually result from a society's very growth and prosperity: the increase in numbers of its membership, the extension of the territory served, the growing magnitude and complexity of its business operations, coupled with the natural inclination, if all this is going well, to leave things in the hands of the management.

These factors are constantly tending, not only to reduce the attendance at general meetings relative to the total membership, but also to take many members beyond their depth in discussion. Opinions are less well grounded, judgement impaired, criticism blunted. While remaining democratic in form, a society becomes steadily less so in fact and in spirit and may end by accepting minority rule as normal or inevitable. This decline is sometimes accelerated by short-sighted management boards, which submit over-optimistic or self-justificatory reports in order to avoid awkward questions or acute controversy, and by officials, under-educated in Co-operative Principles, who regard democratic procedures as a kind of functionless excrescence on their society's business organisation. External factors, such as the attractions of commercialised entertainment, and television, which inclines people to stay at home, also militate against the effectiveness of the general meeting by offering powerful counter-attractions.

The application of the Principle of Democracy in primary Co-operative societies therefore demands, besides constant vigilance and determination to correct weakness and weed out abuses, the continued adaptation and evolution of their democratic organs in harmony with their members' changing circumstances, outlook and wants, as well as their own development. The effort to maximise the conscious participation of the members in the life of the society can never therefore be safely relaxed. They must be continually called upon for contributions of vital significance, not simply to register formal approval of what is done in their name. Co-operative practice in more than one country provides plenty of evidence that, compared with the Movement's business expansion, its democracy is backward, receiving reluctant and inadequate attention, mainly because its application to large-scale enterprises is beset with difficulties. These difficulties are often enhanced by false assumptions as, for example, that the agenda of a Co-operative general meeting must run on the same lines as a shareholders' meeting in a joint-stock company. Of course, the members are shareholders, but their main interest in their society is not in their shareholding or what small return that yields them, but its efficiency in promoting their economic interests as producers or consumers. Marcel Brot,[1] bearing in mind his experience as president of the Union of Co-operators of Lorraine, the largest of France's great regional consumer

Co-operatives, insisted for years that the proper approach to the members is not as shareholders but as users of goods and services. The publicity of his society never allows its members, its employees or the general public to forget that it is the largest association of consumers in France.

What Albert Thomas called the 'sensory apparatus' of the Co-operative Movement has democratic as well as economic functions, if it is used to ascertain and express the general will of the membership, in particular with regard to the kinds of economic service the members desire their society to render. In a secondary degree it can be used to ascertain whether the society is achieving its objects by serving the members to their entire satisfaction. If this had been properly understood and acted upon a generation ago, consumer Co-operatives in particular would have been able to develop and even anticipate the results of what is today fashionably called consumer research. Conversely, it is thoroughly anti-democratic to rule out, as often happens, the discussion of the society's performance and services from the agenda of the general meeting, because this prevents the members from making the best and most active contribution they are competent to make. The most notable examples of successful general meetings under contemporary conditions are those in which there is a friendly confrontation of members and management, with uninhibited discussion of the society's operations, policies and problems.

A Co-operative society's expansion beyond a certain point brings about a transformation of the general meeting or, if it does not, should do so. Membership seldom grows so large that, if any large proportion desired to exercise its right to attend the general meeting, even the local sport stadium would not hold the crowd. When a Co-operative evolves from local to regional dimensions, distance from the centre may tend to disenfranchise some, perhaps the majority, of the members. For a time it may be practicable to hold a series of area meetings with identical agenda and procedures and to obtain decisions by aggregating the votes cast for and against particular proposals. In the long run, however, this solution is rarely satisfactory and the simple general meeting open to all has to be replaced by a representative assembly which exercises the same constitutional functions. But who shall choose the representatives? Obviously, the members themselves. This requires a structure of local groupings usually based in consumers' societies on the network of branch stores, and not too large for members and candidates to be personally known to one another. The pioneers of German consumers' Co-operation recognised the necessity of such a structure and built it into the great urban societies they founded in the early years of this century. At a later stage in 1928, an amendment of the fundamental Co-operative Law made representative assemblies obligatory in all societies whose membership exceeded 3,000 persons. The German example powerfully influenced the constitutional development of consumers' societies in Northern and Central European countries. Quite independently, the great regional consumers' societies of France worked out similar structures. Normally societies consist, at the base, of local 'cells' or 'sections' whose organs are a general meeting; a small committee maintaining contact between members and the general administration but not interfering with the management of the store; and representatives in the general assembly and possibly on the council of supervision of the society. It is significant that in Western Germany this pattern survived the suppression of the consumers' societies by the Hitler Government in 1941. Preserved in the recollection and experience of the Co-operators who were called upon to rebuild their societies after 1945, it made an enormous contribution to the rapid revival of societies' sense of corporate unity in the 1950's.

A more recent and remarkable example is presented by the consumers' Co-operative Movement in Austria because it demonstrates what is possible. The original consumers' Co-operatives were dissolved, like the German, when the country came under Nazi rule, but after freedom was restored, the Movement's revival took the form of regional development in which the system of local members' councils was included. Consolidation ultimately resulted in the promotion of a national Co-operative society, Coop Austria, into which the regional societies with their local councils were absorbed. Simultaneously, constant efforts were made to increase individual membership, while maintaining members' interest by publishing a lively monthly magazine, *Wir von Konsum*. The total membership of Coop Austria now exceeds 800,000. The aggregate attendance at the 1983 local meetings of members was 110,000. The educational and social organisation by which the degree of member participation is secured and maintained will be described later.

Obviously, inscribing 'one member, one vote' in the rule book does not ensure that a Co-operative will be democratically administered. Every society, whether it has a score of members or a million, needs democracy in the form of a continuous, cyclical process consisting of information, discussion (or consultation), decision, execution (or action) and accounting (or reporting). Members must be adequately informed of the matters under consideration. Discussion should be relevant and be allowed sufficient time. Decision may be by voting, which should be unquestionably fair. Execution, or other action consequent on decision, should be entrusted to the appropriate personnel, such as the society's officers. Their report accounting for their actions (or inaction) completes the cycle and they form part of the information which starts another going.

Another series of constitutional problems involving democracy arises from the fact that, as Co-operative societies grow, the functions of their governing organs become increasingly professionalised. By this is meant that some functions can no longer be completely discharged in their spare time by elected persons with a modicum of common sense, honesty and devotion to duty, but must be entrusted to full-time officials with the appropriate talents, special training and experience. The story of the primary society in its pioneer stage, whose committee-members individually and collectively perform all necessary tasks, including service behind the counter, is familiar in almost every country. It was re-enacted when the newly-founded consumers' society Syn-ka began business in Athens in 1963. In the debutante society it is the management of the store, in the more developed the management of the society's business as a whole, which is extruded from the functions of directly elected bodies. They may still retain the titles of management committees or boards of directors, but the function of management slips farther and farther out of their hands as the society grows. After serving five years as the virtually full-time president of a large consumers' society, the author's father once remarked that it was inconceivable that a Co-operative retail enterprise with a turnover of millions of pounds sterling per annum could be in any real sense managed by a group of people, however able, in their spare time. It may be added that the efforts of excessively but mistakenly conscientious committees to retain or recover management functions may be a hindrance to progess and, in certain circumstances, disastrous.

There is a fundamental distinction between the functions of management and those of representing the general will of the members and safeguarding their interests. This was very clearly recognised, for example, in the Co-operative Law of Germany. Even the smallest of German Co-operatives has two organs: the *Vorstand* or management board and the *Aufsichtsrat* or supervisory council. The latter is directly nominated and elected by the members. The former is chosen as a whole by the supervisory council and submitted to the approval of the general meeting which may reject the board proposed but not nominate alternative members, either individually or collectively. The same distinction between policy-making and management was emphasised by the Report of the British Co-operative Independent Commission.[2] The more highly technical management becomes, the less it is possible to invoke democracy in order to defend amateur or lay interference. The members, whose satisfaction is the purpose of the Co-operative's existence, or their representatives are surely entitled to pass an opinion on the results, but hardly qualified to pronounce on the methods by which they are achieved, unless these are at variance with Co-operative Principles or the society's objects.

In the long run it would appear that the functions of the primitive management committee must all be transferred to professionals, save that of representing the members' interests. Yet the larger the primary society grows, and especially when it has burst local bounds and become regional, the more important and exacting the retained functions become.

Unless the committee maintains touch with the members so that it can keep aware of their changing moods and circumstances, faithfully interpreting their wishes and anticipating their needs, it cannot effectively guide the management in its business policies and its general approaches to the members. Member and public relations eventually become the committee's (or council's) principal field of responsibility and work.

Moreover, the elected council of members (whether called supervisory or not), especially if it is the body which nominates or appoints the management, has essential rights: to be informed, to advise and to warn. It may even represent the society as employer in relation to its chief officials. The management board, where the council is alert and active, wields no absolute power even in management. In many important situations it cannot do without the positive support of the council. Vital issues of business policy, embarkation on far-reaching schemes of development, important investments or property purchases require the information of and consultation with the council beforehand. The society's rules may also specify matters which require the consent or agreement of both bodies or decision in a joint meeting. To sum up, the welfare and success of the large Co-operatives necessitated by present and future competitive conditions require the careful and precise articulation of their organs of representation and management, so as to maintain equilibrium, ensure mutual respect for authority, avoid friction and maximise the effectiveness of the structure as a whole. Conversely, where any of the organs are weak, disabled or in any way unable to discharge their functions, dislocation is the immediate and atrophy may be the ultimate consequence, as anyone knows who has a broken limb. Efficiency, in the sense in which Co-operation demands it, is not the concern of business management alone. As Marcel Brot has again and again emphasised, management cannot reach its highest pitch of efficiency unless Democracy is also efficient.

Although Co-operative administration may, nay must, be democratic, is there no place for Democracy in management? In the final analysis yes, but the practical difficulties which beset its realisation are often enormous and are not to be surmounted by Co-operators insufficiently schooled in democratic discipline. One type of Co-operative organisation, the workers' productive or labour society, since it is essentially an attempt by workers to become collectively their own employers, is a deliberate effort to implant democracy in management. Success is by no means easily, still less invariably, achieved. Many productive societies, in order to preserve their existence as enterprises, have been obliged to sacrifice their democratic, i.e. their Co-operative character. Those which have been so fortunate as to achieve both Co-operative and business success, owe it very largely to wise, far-sighted and unselfish leadership and possibly also to the fact that Co-operation in the broader sense is indispensable to efficiency in modern industry. The more elaborate division of labour becomes in industrial organisation the more must success depend on team-work, the essence of which is a united will for a common objective. It is generally accepted that good personnel management consists in the evocation and maintenance of a powerful team-spirit within the enterprise. In order to do this it is necessary to cease thinking of the enterprise as — in the words of Karl Marx — a machine which consists of human beings, but rather to regard it as a society capable of possessing a general will, as that has been defined earlier in this chapter. There is thus no necessary or inevitable antithesis between management and democracy, but rather the possibility of reconciliation on a deeper level than most industrial organisation has yet reached. The workers' productive societies are not pursuing a chimera.

But what of the consumers' and agricultural Co-operatives as well as the other types which are employers of various kinds of workers, some of them in large numbers? Do not the employees of any such Co-operative constitute in fact a society, a community of interests, within the Co-operative? If so, do they not possess democratic rights of consultation, representation and decision? How are these rights to be reconciled with the democracy and good management of the Co-operative? For the Co-operators of the pioneer era, these questions scarcely existed or could be postponed, as employees were not numerous. For the most part Co-operative employment accepted the ordinary wage contract of private enterprise under which the wage-earner and many a salary-earner had no voice in management. In many a consumers' Co-operative, employees, although admitted to membership to the extent of purchasing in the store and receiving dividend on their purchases, might not even vote in elections for management committees. In agricultural Co-operatives employees, if not themselves farmers, were usually not eligible for membership at all. As the employees had no rights recognised within the constitutions of the societies, they had no alternative to asserting them and negotiating on their employment conditions extra-constitutionally through trade unions. On the whole the Co-operative Movement was content to wait for the change in public opinion in favour of workers' representation in management, and even for legislation enacting it, before seriously seeking to solve problems inherent in its own Principle of Democracy — problems growing in importance with the increasing numbers of its commercial and industrial personnel.

There would soon be two distinct series of problems concerned respectively with self-determination and with participation in management and control. The claim to self-determination is founded on the fact that the workers as a body have common concerns affecting their work and welfare in which employers are not interested in the same way or degree and in which consumers may not be interested at all. Particular groups of workers also have special interests different from those other groups, a fact that underlies the traditional trade union 'chapel' organisation of the printing trade. A democratic structure for an enterprise or an industry must therefore recognise the existence of functional groups of workers and allow each powers of self-determination, corresponding and limited to the special interests and responsibilities of its members, relating to the organisation, classification, recruitment and training of labour; remuneration and promotion; the hygiene of the workplace and other conditions affecting workers' welfare. Such a structure would of course be ineffective if the workers' groups did not possess to a considerable degree a sense of collective responsibility, not simply for the defence of their interests, but also for the efficient performance of their work and collaboration with other groups. In so far as the groups prove themselves capable of wise and effective determination, the function of management in a democratic system would tend to become more and more the co-ordination of group activity according to agreed plans and programmes. This may seem a distant ideal, human nature being what it is, but here and there, in both the past and present, it has been partly realised in practice. Dr Georges Fauquet in his time called attention to the collective contract system adopted in the French national printing establishment, under which groups of workers contracted collectively with the management for the performance of a given piece of work at an agreed price and determined each worker's remuneration according to their own rules and standards. It is regrettable that the absorption in 1964 of the joint enterprise of producers and consumers, the Laiteries Réunies,[3] by the consumers' Co-operative of Geneva involved the dissolution of the roundsmen's *Communauté* which for many years had carried out collective contracts with the Laiteries Réunies for the house-to-house delivery of milk and fixed the individual pay and working conditions of its members.

Participation involves almost invariably, but not exclusively, representation on managing or supervisory authorities, i.e. policy-making bodies. The employees are not usually content for long with merely consultative rights and powers exercised through works councils or similar organs, unless these are also represented in the supreme administrative authority in the society.

A sign of the times was the legal recognition of the workers' right to join in policy-making (*Mitbestimmungsrecht*) in the Federal German Republic. The system is probably not entirely satisfactory from either the management's or the workers' point of view, but it is capable of adjustment and improvement, if there is general willingness to learn from experience. In any case the admission in principle of participation marks an important step in the direction of democracy. Further progress depends upon the just and skilful delimitation of functions and authority, so that the various communities of interest are articulated in a manner conducive to collaboration and therefore to efficiency. The greatest danger is always the assumption by any organ of the absolute or final authority (which should reside in the whole membership of a society) or of the competence or functions of any other organ. Equilibrium, which need not be either static or rigid, must be the constant aim.

Failure to keep this necessity clearly in mind is the key to the disappointing performance in recent years of some large-scale consumers' Co-operatives in which neglect of democratic constitutional development has more or less directly retarded economic progress. A common source of disequilibrium appears to be a decline in the authority and effectiveness of the general meeting. It is not simply that the general meeting does not evolve into a representative assembly with supporting local groupings, as described earlier, but that its decline has been hastened by the dullness and empty formality of its proceedings. The first general meeting attended by the writer as a new member of a consumers' society in Manchester in the 1920's completed its agenda — having approved the report of the management committee, the accounts and balance sheet, elected new members to the management and education committees and passed two or three routine resolutions — in 12 minutes.

Of course, where group and party differences give rise to controversy, a certain liveliness can be imparted to the proceedings, but this kind of interest soon palls and dwindling attendances can well set off a deplorable chain-reaction. The shrinking field of selection for elective offices leads sooner or later to a deterioration in the quality of the officers, particularly in the membership of the management committee or board of directors. Where these prove incapable of giving wise and courageous leadership, authority and power often pass to the chief permanent officials. The committee, instead of being the mouthpiece of the membership, tends to become the management's chief apologist. Lacking the spur of intelligent and constructive criticism, the management in turn is inclined to be unenterprising and routine-minded.

This functional dislocation is aggravated where the general meeting is largely monopolised by mainly self-interested groups contending for sectional advantage. Their faction-fighting dissipates energy, distracts attention from vital, long-term issues and reduces democratic procedures to empty farce. This situation is not remedied by well-meant but only half-enlightened efforts to correct the inferior position of employees dating, as already mentioned, from the early days of the Movement. As it seemed harsh and illogical to deprive the employees of their rights as consumers because they happened to be employed by a consumers' Co-operative society, they were given the same rights as other members to vote for and be elected to the committee of management. It thus became possible for the employees, as an organised group, not merely to dominate the general meeting but to secure a majority on the management committee. Theoretically this stands the fundamental idea of consumers' Co-operation on its head. Practically it often leads, as might well be expected, to a lack of consistency and determination in protecting consumers' interests; a lack of ruthlessness in weeding out inefficiency and introducing reforms required for efficiency if these might lead to dismissals; and failure of the committee fully to support the officials in disciplinary matters and in other ways when prompt and drastic action may be necessary or salutary. None of these deficiencies needs arise if there is at all times in the society a nucleus of consumer members actively and intelligently interested, large enough to overpower the minorities or in certain circumstances a coalition of minorities. Neglect to maintain and encourage such a nucleus amounts to a betrayal, for it is the indispensable condition of Democracy's existence and continuance in Co-operative affairs.

The application of Democracy in the constitution and working of federations of Co-operatives must necessarily differ from its application in primary societies, but most of the special problems it creates have been solved long ago by the common sense and experience of Co-operators. Differences in size between society-members make the rule of one member, one vote inappropriate. To give a vast metropolitan consumers' society with hundreds of thousands of members and a village society with a hundred members or less each a single vote would be unfair to the point of absurdity. The one notable case in Co-operative history where failure to admit this split a Co-operative Movement in two has already been mentioned in Chapter One. Of course, in this example the issue at stake was more than mere voting rights; it was the distribution of power in the Movement's national organisation and it was aggravated by cleavages of social and political outlook between the contending groups. Differential voting power has long been recognised as the only practical solution, and the proof of its widespread acceptance is seen in its adoption in the rules of the International Co-operative Alliance and a host of other federations. The usual method is to allot each member-organisation one basic vote and additional votes according to a sliding scale, based more or less directly on membership: behind the organisations stand larger or smaller groups or persons.

Obviously where differences in size are very great, a ceiling must be fixed for the number of votes allotted to the largest member-organisations, otherwise a few of them could too easily dominate a federation or pay too little regard to the rights or views of the smaller members. In the ICA not only is such a ceiling imposed by rule, but the constitution also provides that no single national member may exercise more than one seventh of the voting power in the International Co-operative Congress which is the general assembly of the Alliance. This recognises the need, not only to provide effectively channels for Democracy to manifest itself positively, but also to adopt adequate safeguards against undemocratic decisions or actions.

The constitutions of Co-operative federations also illustrate in other ways the concern to attract and encourage the intelligent interest of individual Co-operators in whose name, in the last analysis, all their operations are carried on. Most federations of national dimensions, even if they did not originate in collaboration between pre-existing regional federations, develop a regional substructure intended to bridge the gap between their central administration and their members. In large countries like India or the Soviet Union with federal constitutions, this structure may include an additional tier corresponding to the federal states. In European national federations, it is normal for the congresses or general assemblies to be preceded by a series of general meetings of their regional sub-federations, when representatives of the national body present reports on its activity and sound out opinion on various questions which are expected to come up for their final decision at the national assembly or congress. This system enables more local delegates to participate than could attend the national congress. At the same time it enables the attendance at the congress to be kept down to the number appropriate to an effective deliberative assembly. Nevertheless, it also tends to reduce certain functions of the national assembly to the formal registration of decisions already made elsewhere, because by the close of the series of regional meetings, the trend of opinion on most of the questions posed will have already been clearly indicated and become generally known (unlike the British Congress where decisions on important issues sometimes cannot be forecast with certainty and the assembly seethes with tension and excitement until the result of the voting is declared). The congress or national assembly is not therefore redundant. On the contrary, it provides opportunities for the wider surveys, the airing of new ideas and suggestions, the exposition of plans and programmes for the future that contemporary competitive conditions make more than ever necessary. Congresses, if they may have lost some of the excitements of debate, have enlarged their educational functions. They could well increase their value and importance still further if the need is borne in mind for creating and animating among Co-operators a national consciousness, without which a national federation has nothing which corresponds to a 'general will'.

In this connection the more or less successful efforts of certain American Co-operative organisations, especially in the field of insurance, to diffuse a sense of participation among widely scattered groups of Co-operators, are worthy of note. Mutual Service Co-operative, St Paul, Minnesota, is an organisation created by Co-operatives of various types and by a large number of local mutual insurance associations, which are joint owners of two mutual institutions, one for life and the other for casualty insurance. Mutual Service Co-operative exercises on their behalf the powers of control inherent in the policy-holders and their participating Co-operative and mutual organisations, by electing the directors and determining the business aims and policies of the two institutions. It is itself governed by its member-bodies, regional and local, each of which possesses one vote. Its constitution provides for an allocation of functions between central, regional and local bodies and enumerates their mutual obligations. The powers and duties of the local participating Co-operative, for example, include the contribution of $10 to the capital of Mutual Service Co-operative in order to acquire the right to vote; the endorsement of the Mutual Service Insurance institutions and their recommendation to its own members; representation by one delegate at annual and other meetings where controlling powers are exercised; practical assistance to the two institutions in bringing their services to the attention of its members; and participation in programmes and projects at a local level.

The Nationwide group of insurance institutions in the USA is sponsored by nine farmers' and Co-operative organisations which nominate candidates for election to the board of directors. The large number of policy-holders who are members of the sponsoring organisations may bring influence to bear on both the elections and the policies favoured by the board. But in addition, and particularly with the object of bringing in other policy-holders, Nationwide has constituted an advisory committee in which some 20,000 policy-holders take part. Nationwide agents set up local groups of policy-holders to discuss the services and problems of the organisation. The groups appoint representatives to district meetings whose recommendations are forwarded to headquarters. Representatives of district and regional groups are assembled periodically at Columbus, Ohio, for a three-day conference, with all the officers of Nationwide in attendance. In a final plenary session recommendations may be adopted for direct submission to the management. Each of these systems of participation has its merits and limitations, but they illustrate the possibilities of infusing with a democratic spirit institutions which, constituted by bodies which are frequently federations themselves, are often remote from the direct influence of rank and file Co-operators dependent on their services.

Evidently, the structure of the Co-operative Movement today, expanding in accordance with the principles of Unity and Democracy, imposes a continually increasing burden of responsibility upon the individual men and women who become members and possibly officers of Co-operative societies. Sooner or later, directly or remotely, all that is attempted or accomplished by Co-operative organisations — local, national and international — is reported to them for their judgement or approval. To understand what he is told, the typical Co-operator of this century must be conscious on all three of these levels, and consciousness includes not merely being aware but also forming opinions and expressing wishes which may harden into decisions. If he is not equal to making needful decisions, others will decide for him and, as the Movement's functions become more and more professionalised with its growing extent and complexity, it will be its bureaucrats or technocrats, rather than Democracy, who will save it from confusion and ultimate decline.

There is no single constitutional prescription for Democracy, any more than there is for health. But just as the conditions for healthy living are known, so also are the conditions in which Democracy can live and flourish. Most of these conditions depend on the observance of Co-operative Principles, some already, some to be, discussed. If we limit our discussion to the mere mechanism of democratic government, the reality may still elude us. For in Dr Fauquet's words, Democracy does not exist save as a moral climate in which decisions are made.

CHAPTER FIVE

Equity

The Rochdale Pioneers proclaimed their Society to be 'equitable' by including that word in its title. Their example was followed by more than a few other groups of British Co-operators of the first generation. One of the oldest and best known of the English workers' productive societies bears the title Equity Shoes to this day. The idea of Equity and its practical realisation were clearly of great importance to these pioneers. The meaning they attached to the term is not the jurist's, who has to rectify divergences of law from natural justice; nor yet the businessman's, who is concerned with the rights of shareholders to the profits of joint-stock companies, but rather that distributive aspect of justice, briefly discussed by the ancient Greek philosopher Aristotle in Book V of the *Nicomachaean Ethics*, which is involved in the exchange of the products of one man's labour against those of another's.

The early Co-operators were obliged to consider Equity in two different but related ways, which may be roughly contrasted as theoretical and practical. On the one hand, with the theoretical, they were concerned with equity — even more perhaps with inequity — in the distribution of income and wealth in society at large. On the other hand, with the practical, they were concerned with the distribution in an equitable manner among its members of the economic benefits yielded by any Co-operative society. The more they convinced themselves that the distribution of wealth in the economic system in general was inequitable, the more they were bound to devise a system of sharing the profits and other advantages of Co-operative association which the members as a whole should accept as equitable. Failing the formulation and application of such a system, unity would be undermined by discontent and might prove impossible to maintain.

The situation of the working classes in Great Britain is acknowledged to be a classic case and it was more or less parallel in country after country as the Industrial Revolution spread across Europe. When the first ventures in Co-operation were made, the enormous increase in productivity which accompanied the introduction of the new industrial techniques had not yet appreciably benefited the wage-earners and their families. For about a century it had the effect of increasing the inequalities in wealth and income between the different social classes. The displaced handicraftsmen, smallholders and farm workers who migrated to the new industrial settlements in search of employment were in an inferior bargaining position when wages came to be fixed. As individuals they were powerless and had to accept what wages a prospective employer saw fit to offer. When they tried collective bargaining, or 'combination' as it was then called, they were rarely successful and when in desperation they declared a strike, their families more than half-starved for they had neither individual savings nor collective funds to support them.

The workers had not yet learned discipline and their violence gave the authorities an excuse for suppressing their trade unions. Their leaders were mostly untrained and inexperienced in organisation and negotiation. The employers often refused to recognise the unions and wrecked or suppressed them when they could. For about a quarter of a century, between 1799 and 1824, the unions were actually illegal. On the other hand a single large employer who could offer jobs to scores or perhaps hundreds of workers was, in the words of the economist Nassau Senior,[1] 'a combination in himself.' In these circumstances the Iron Law of Wages inevitably operated and the workers' earnings tended to sink towards subsistence level rather than to rise with labour's increasing productivity, the yield of which was intercepted by the entrepreneur. The shrewder and more enlightened among the workers understood this very well and they resented bitterly not only the inequality but still more the injustice of such a division of the product of industry.

The workers' sentiments were rationalised for them by a whole school of critics of the orthodox political economy of the day. These fastened in particular upon the labour theory of value, and from the proposition that the exchange value of commodities is determined by the relative quantities of labour entering into their production they drew the conclusion that labour was the sole source of wealth. Accordingly, those who lived upon rent, interest and profits contributed nothing to production to justify the incomes they drew from it and were exploiting the real producers. The institution of private property, the penal system by which it was protected, the State itself, were simply means by which the well-to-do maintained a distribution of income and possessions which was based on robbery.

The Irish landowner, William Thompson, who described himself as living on 'rent, the product of the labour of others' became a leading exponent of Robert Owen's community scheme for the precise reason that the workers, when organised in communities, would retain for themselves the whole produce of their labour. The same idea underlay the workers' Co-operative productive society and other social experiments of the 1820's and Thompson advocated it in his celebrated address to the silk-weavers of Spitalfields. It was later taken over by Karl Marx to become one of the foundations of his social doctrine. How far the Rochdale Pioneers were directly influenced by these ideas there is now little evidence to show, but it is hard to believe that they were not debated by the discussion society in the Owenite reading room from which the Pioneers' Society ultimately sprang. In any event, the Pioneers, like many other working people, yearned to emancipate themselves from an industrial and social order that was fundamentally inequitable and to join in creating a better society in which social justice should reign.

There was, however, one other factor which helped to deny the wage earners their proper share of increased productivity. That was the failure of the distributive trade, wholesale and retail, to keep pace with industry in modernising its organisation and methods. At any given level of earnings, the industrial proletariat depended for its standard of living upon the purchasing power of money wages, in other words the level of rents and retail prices.

The technological changes which transformed industry had scarcely any counterpart in distributive trade until the advent of the multiple store towards the close of the 19th century indicated that some of the lessons of large scale economic organisation were being learned and applied. Retailing especially remained individualistic, inefficient, conservative of old ways and traditions, and not over-honest in respect of the purity and quality of goods, in particular foodstuffs. In the new industrial settlements the shop-keepers earned their living too easily by exploiting the workers' families. Even though, in a period of unemployment or a labour dispute, the shop-keepers might allow them credit to keep the wolf from the door, that service was greatly outweighed by the virtually permanent burden of debt carried by many families. Here again, as consumers, the wage-earners were in a weak bargaining position until they turned to Co-operation as a means of controlling retail distribution and achieving Equity by fixing prices which represented real costs rather than inflated values.

The urgent need of working-class households in 'the hungry 40's' for immediate economic relief largely accounts for one important difference between the consumers' Co-operative Movement after Rochdale and the earlier movement between 1828 and 1834 inspired and guided by Dr William King's *Co-operator*. Dr King assumed that the surplus resulting from trade and production would be accumulated by the Co-operative society as a capital fund for the self-supporting community into which it would ultimately evolve. There is no record of any society which advanced so far, but it is well-known that many tried one method or another of dividing profits, whether an equal share to every member or a share reckoned according to capital contributed or, in one or two cases, according to purchases. It is not recorded that any considerable group of the Rochdale Pioneers favoured the capitalisation rather than the division of the profits of their projected society. Their problem was to formulate and agree upon a system of division. Their solution, if not original, became historic. Yet it has been studied and discussed much more in respect of its business advantages as an inducement to join the society and purchase consistently from the store than as part of the application of the Principle of Equity. Even the ICA Committee of the 1930's seems not to have fully appreciated the relation of the dividend on purchases system to fixed interest on share capital and the price policy adopted by the Pioneers from this point of view.

It is significant that the ICA Commission on the Principles, reporting after the distributive revolution had been some years under way, while recommending that Co-operatives should be to a considerable degree self-financing, declared that interest rates should be limited but not fixed, and rather elastic. In other words, interest should be limited but the rate should not be determined by a rule which could be amended only by a meeting subject to six weeks' notice, but should follow the general trend of interest rates, rather like the building societies.

Of course, if a Co-operative has no capital or does not pay interest — and there are such — there is no problem. But in societies where membership implies capital holding and interest is paid upon it, the rate of interest must be deliberately held below the rate which would be regarded as fair at any given time in the ordinary market, or at least not exceed the ordinary bank rate of discount or some other rate regarded as a fair return. Theoretically the holder of capital is not entitled to any element of profit or surplus, which belongs to the consumer or worker.

The Commission nevertheless foresaw the possibility of a society, needing more capital than could be raised in this way, being tempted to break the rule by offering, under competitive conditions, higher rates than the rule would justify. Unfortunately the tendency has been rather in the opposite direction. Too many societies have been too slow to raise their interest rates, thus depriving themselves of the means of effectively meeting competition by self-financing. Today the advertisement columns of the newspapers reveal only too plainly what competition for investment capital Co-operatives have to meet, and it is conceivable that some of them are already too late to take effective action. The Commission even envisaged the time when local or regional self-financing would be inadequate and the Movement would depend even more than it does at present on national institutions which themselves may be obliged to borrow outside the Movement. Meanwhile, it is important that societies' interest rates should be raised to the minimum which is effectively competitive.

It may avoid misunderstanding to remark here that Equity, as understood for the purpose of the present discussion, implies no kind of obligation on any kind of Co-operative society to divide the whole or any part of its profits or surplus among its members. The Raiffeisen type of credit society would keep its accumulated surpluses undivided, even at its own dissolution. Many Co-operators maintain that on a society's dissolution no member can equitably claim a share of its surplus assets, if any. Under the strict Raiffeisen system of Co-operative credit the rule has always required that the surplus assets of a dissolved society shall be applied to purposes benefiting the whole community, not its members alone. The Rochdale Pioneers, in amended Rules adopted in October 1854, laid down that, if their Society came to be dissolved, 'the surplus, if any, of (its) property shall be applied by the trustees for the time being of the Society to such charitable or public purposes as they think fit'. Or the farmers' supply society, which gives its members the advantage of buying seeds, fertilisers and other farm requisites at approximately cost-price, is not necessarily less equitable or Co-operative than the consumers' society which pays out most of its surplus in dividends on purchases (patronage refunds).

The Principle of Equity is not infringed by those societies which give the member the option of an immediate discount for cash or waiting until the year's end for the normal dividend. On the other hand, the practice of consumers' societies in the Soviet Union and some other Communist-ruled countries making no other division of surplus than the payment of dividends on shareholdings is dubious and a departure from Principle, whatever arguments from expediency may be brought to defend or excuse it. The point is that if the members choose to keep their society's surplus undivided, no one is entitled to condemn them; but if there is division, the only equitable method is according to the individual member's turnover with the society, after interest on shares has been set aside.

Confusion arises from the habit of regarding the payment of dividend on turnover as the chief object, the *raison d'être* of a Co-operative (as a company normally aims at dividends on its capital) rather than as a by-product of its successful operation. The High Court of the Federal German Republic, in a discriminating judgement handed down in 1963, rightly declared that dividend on turnover represented not a commercial profit, but the economic benefit which the members obviously seek by joining or forming their Co-operative. This, however, does not mean that the economic benefit must always take the form of a dividend or that the society cannot confer advantages on its members which are additional or alternative to it. Indeed, with changing competitive conditions and, especially, diminishing gross profit margins, the dividend as a form of economic benefit seems destined for a role of dwindling importance — a question to be discussed in another connection later in this chapter.

To return to the Rochdale formula we may observe that the Pioneers, having decided to aim at a surplus by selling at market prices, had to take into account two different interests — those of the purchasers whose spending in the store constituted the Society's revenue and those of the shareholders who provided the capital without which it could not set up in business at all. These parties were, of course, the members acting in two different capacities. The solution adopted by the Pioneers was based on distinctions which had not yet become clear even to the professional economists of their day — the distinction between the capitalist and the entrepreneur and the consequent distinction between interest and profit. The Pioneers do not appear to have questioned the premise that capital enhances productivity or the claim of those who contribute capital to be paid for its use at rates of interest normal under prevailing conditions. They were not entitled to more, as the functions of the entrepreneur rightly belong to the members in their other capacity as consumers or purchasers. Interest having been calculated, the surplus remaining accrued to the members as partners in the business and the only fair principle of division was according to their purchases. Allocations to reserves and other common purposes may be left out of account for the moment as they are not involved in this aspect of Equity.

It has more than once been observed, however, that the payment of a uniform dividend on purchases ignores the difference in profit margins for different classes of goods. Experiments are made from time to time with differential dividends or no dividends at all for special categories of goods or services, but they have never brought about any general modification in practice and have more often than not been abandoned, after longer or shorter experience, as being too troublesome or expensive to calculate. Uniformity remains the rule.

It is not claimed on behalf of the Pioneers' formula that it was an example of perfect Equity, nor would there be any point in doing so, were it possible. The formula was fair enough to satisfy the bulk of their members and of the generations of consumer Co-operators who followed them. It has rarely been seriously challenged. This is not by implication to dismiss, as lacking in seriousness, the objections of numerous Co-operators to the payment of interest on the minimum shareholding required for full membership rights. But, except in so far as a Co-operative organisation can put aside non-interest-bearing capital from its own revenues, it is obliged to hire capital either from its members or from outsiders, e.g. banks and insurance institutions, at interest rates determined by the state of the capital market, the security offered, the period of repayment and other conditions. Most Co-operators therefore accept interest as a practical necessity which the Movement must accept until it grows powerful enough to do without it.

Parallel considerations apply to the just price. The Rochdale Pioneers and many others since their time have had to accept prices reached by the higgling of the market until they grew powerful enough to impose fairer or more stable prices in the interests of their associated consumers or producers. At times, objection has been raised to rates of interest as unnecessarily high, thus reducing the amount of disposable surplus, and to the use of the society for investment purposes by non-purchasing members. The practice of paying lower rates of interest on the shares of members whose purchases failed to exceed a prescribed minimum was at one time fairly widespread among consumers' societies in the North of England. At the beginning and for a considerable period afterwards the Pioneers' distribution problem was not complicated. Labour, in the persons of the Society's employees — Samuel Ashworth, the first shopkeeper, and his assistants — was not a claimant to a share of surplus. Consumer Co-operators were content to pay the wages then prevailing for shop and office workers and trade union rates for skilled craftsmen. For over two generations, the whole consumers' Co-operative Movement benefited from the fact that distribution was one of the industries characterised by low wage rates.

Nevertheless, the labour theory of value and the workers' claim to the whole product of their labour were by no means dead or done with. The workers' Co-operative productive societies promoted by the Christian Socialists and their successors were attempts at industrial organisation on lines which would enable the associated workers after paying the rent of their premises, interest on capital, salaries and wages at normal rates, to dispose of any surplus by adding it to capital or dividing it among themselves on any basis they considered equitable, such as the numbers of hours each member had worked.

The entry of the consumers' societies and their wholesales into production touched off a controversy which raged for over 20 years and in the end died away without being finally resolved. On one side, the advocates of productive societies, without challenging the right of consumers to dispose of the whole surplus accruing from distribution, contended that workers in productive enterprises had the right to at least a share, if not the whole, of its profits. To which the defenders of the consumers' organisations retorted that the distinction between production and distribution drawn by their opponents was false. Distribution, since it added use-values to the products of industry by making them available where and when and in what quantities they were required by consumers, was not essentially different from production but in fact the latter's final stage. They were also able to refute the doctrine of the workers' claim to the whole product because economic science had rejected the labour theory of value in favour of the marginal utility theory. In other words, the determinant of value was to be found on the demand side and not the supply side of the market. And in any case, they maintained, the workers were able as members of consumers' societies to share in the surpluses.

Despite this theoretical deadlock, many of the consumers' societies and most of the workers' productive societies in Great Britain adopted compromise solutions. Many consumer Co-operators felt that the crude wage system prevailing in ordinary private enterprise, especially in the distributive trade, was inconsistent with Co-operative ideals and therefore unworthy of the Movement, which should show itself to be a more humane and generous employer than the hard-fisted man. Scores of retail societies and the Scottish Co-operative Wholesale Society paid their employees from the surplus a regular bonus in addition to their wages. The English Co-operative Wholesale Society, however, after trying different bonus schemes, quickly abandoned them on the grounds that it could not devise a uniform scheme that would be equitable for all the varied classes of worker it employed in production and distribution and it became the chief defender of the consumers' right to the whole of the surplus where they initiated and controlled a given enterprise. On their side, the workers' societies introduced a similar modification in the opposite direction by admitting their customers, who were very often consumers' Co-operatives, to a share in surplus in the form of a dividend on their purchases. This frequently went along with the admission of consumers' societies to membership, and even included the right of representation on the management board. The result was a blended type of organisation to which the term Co-operative Co-partnership is usually applied and it is characterised by the declaration, at one and the same time, of dividends on purchases and a bonus to labour.

As the present discussion is not concerned with passing judgement on any of the accepted types of Co-operative enterprise but simply with illustrating the importance attached by Co-operators to considerations of Equity and their concern that they should be given due weight, it is desirable to describe briefly some examples from other countries than Great Britain and their producers' as well as consumers' Co-operative Movements. Charles Fourier, who stands in a similar relation to Co-operation in France to that of Robert Owen in Great Britain, had ideas on the distribution of income which influenced one remarkable experiment in consumers' Co-operation and many workers' productive societies. In Fourier's ideal community, in which the members would be at one and the same time producers and consumers, the total revenue should be divided between labour, capital and a third factor which he called 'talent' or management in the ratio 5;4;3. Nine years before the opening of the Pioneers' store in Rochdale a disciple of Fourier, Michel Derrion, founded a consumers' society called Le Commerce Veridique et Social at Lyons. This society, which was in business about three years, divided its surplus on a variant of Fourier's method. The surplus was divided into four equal portions, one of which was allocated to reserve, one distributed among the employees, one assigned to interest on capital, the remaining quarter being divided among the customers in proportion to their purchases. In the first six months of 1836, when the Society was running well, capital's portion was equal to a rate of five per cent on shares, whilst that of the customers was about one and a half per cent on their purchases. The Society's profit margins were deliberately kept low so that it might influence current prices in the consumers' favour. The Society's very success led to its liquidation after three years. The shopkeepers, alarmed by its competition, contrived to bring upon it the suspicion of the authorities by suggesting it was a camouflaged revolutionary association. At the same time they involved Derrion in a lawsuit which ruined him financially and obliged him to leave Lyons.

In the 1840's there were many little grocery shops and bakeries promoted by Fourier's disciples desirous of applying their master's ideas, but there is no historical continuity between them and the French consumers' Co-operative Movement of today, which is based on the Rochdale Principles. Partly as the result of circumstances and partly because of policy, however, the dividend on purchase system in French and many other European consumers' Co-operatives has been somewhat different in its operation from the British, although there is no real difference in principle. Lower standards of living on the Continent caused the members to require from the consumers' societies immediate, tangible advantages in the form of lower prices than were charged by private traders. Co-operative price calculation therefore aimed at a level slightly, but consistently, under market prices. In Great Britain, on the contrary, the Rochdale rule of sale at market-prices was generally observed, but in localities where the Co-operative stores dominated the market there was also a marked tendency for prices to be somewhat above the market level. In periods of high employment and earnings Co-operators did not object to paying higher prices because any excess would be returned later as part of their dividend on purchases. Another factor was the fairly widespread practice, when managements were fixing selling prices, of taking the usual rate of dividend into the reckoning. Whereas it was customary to say that in Britain prices may be a little higher than the market level, but the net price after deducting dividend lower, on the Continent it could be said that prices were lower than the market level in the Co-operative store with the members receiving a dividend in addition.

Dividend rates were on the average lower on the Continent than in Great Britain and in addition, Continental consumers' societies often had no liability for interest on share capital, especially where Socialist ideas were influential. As no interest was paid on shares, the members had no special inducement to take out more than the minimum number or value prescribed by their society's rules. If members entrusted savings to their society they did so in the form of loan deposits on which, of course, they were paid interest. The role of share capital in building up consumers' societies' financial resources in Britain is not paralleled in any other country known to the writer. Conversely, reserves play a more important part on the Continent than in Britain. Allocations to reserve funds from surplus naturally tend to reduce the amount disposable for dividends, but these open reserves are supplemented in all well-managed societies by hidden reserves from liberal depreciation of fixed assets before surplus is declared. Both methods of accumulating reserves of collectively-owned capital are employed, especially at wholesale level. The Swiss and Scandinavian wholesale societies in particular pay little or no dividend on purchases to their affiliated societies but capitalise the bulk of their surplus and devote the rest to various common purposes.

Although these differences of method and practice have considerable interest from the point of view of business technique, they have no great significance from the standpoint of Equity. What arrangement the members of a Co-operative accept as fair among themselves and between the individual members and the society can scarcely be challenged by any outsider. Nevertheless it is interesting to note that, with the passage of time and under the pressure of competition, British and Continental practices tend to approximate to each other. Shrinking trading margins have made it impossible for British societies in general to maintain their traditional high dividend rates. Dividend has lost its potency in comparison with low prices and the quality and presentation of commodities as an attraction to prospective purchasers. On the other hand, the Continental consumers' Co-operative Movements, in order to finance the modernisation of their business structures, equipment and techniques, have been obliged to raise as much capital as possible from their members by raising the value of their shares or the minimum shareholding, or interest rates. Naturally, while the Principle of Equity applies to all the economic benefits offered by a Co-operative to its members, certain of them are at any given time more important than others and with changing times the order of importance can change also.

Turning from consumers' Co-operation, we may now consider some examples of the application of the Principle of Equity in producers' Co-operative Movements. Taking first the practice of the workers' Co-operative productive societies, we may note that Fourier's plan for income distribution mentioned earlier finds echoes in the model rules for such societies issued by their Confédération Générale in France. Article 44 of the rules provides for the division of the net profits, after deduction of the allocation of 15 per cent to reserve required by law, between capital, labour and management (which corresponds to what Fourier called 'talent'). The share of profit assigned to capital is a percentage fixed by rule and by law may never exceed the share allotted to labour. Only paid-up shares rank for dividend. Members whose shares are not yet paid up in full do not draw their interest or their workers' share of profit, but both are credited to their share capital account. Labour's percentage of profit, which by law may not be less that 25 per cent and by custom may be as high as 50 per cent, is also fixed by rule. The sum available is divided among the workers and employees in proportion to the wages or salary earned during the accounting period. Auxiliary workers are included in this distribution, provided that they have worked for the society for at least a month. The participants in the profit allocated to management are the general manager or director and the members of the board of administration whose total and individual shares are percentages of profits fixed by rule. If a society adopts the model rules, the amount of surplus disposable for distribution to members, officials and auxiliaries is reduced not only by the legal reserve, but also by fixed percentages reserved for development and for assistance to members in distress and to a specially constituted fund for retirement pensions. The reserves for development are usually greater in those societies whose industry requires greater amounts of capital per worker.

In those humbler relatives of the skilled workers' productive societies, the labour contracting societies, which are numerous, for example, in Italy, the worker-members' share of surplus is calculated on the number of days he has been employed by the society and the wages he has earned during the accounting period. Employment in these societies is liable to be irregular, varying according to the work in hand, and societies are often not able to employ all their members all the year round. Another circumstance of importance is that, since labour societies operate with a minimum of fixed capital, the claim of capital upon surplus is minimal also. In effect, the principal question to be decided is the relative importance of the claims of the present and the future; in other words, how much the workers shall receive as an immediate supplement to their wages and how much shall be set aside for sickness and unemployment pay, retirement pensions and assistance to widows and orphans, from which the workers or their families may one day benefit.

Conflicting claims between groups of worker-members belonging to different trades or professions are not unknown, although the record of harmonious relations between workers' productive societies and the professional workers they engage is in general very good. An example of the reverse is a dispute which broke out early in 1964 in the workers' productive society at Amiens, France, producing the daily paper *Le Courrier Picard*. The dispute arose on the question of remuneration between the editorial staff and the typographical workers. Thanks to first-class management and favourable local conditions, both groups and, indeed, all the society's worker-members were being paid rates considerably in excess of those fixed by the collective agreements covering their respective trades or professions and higher than those prevailing generally in the Press. After the printers had been granted an advance in wages equal to an award made under the collective agreement for their trade, the journalists demanded a corresponding increase in their salaries. The claim that wage increases granted to one class of worker should be automatically applied to another covered by different collective agreements was not one which the management board, on which the printers were in the majority, was willing to grant. Nevertheless the journalists persisted in their demands. The board was equally firm in its refusal. The ensuing deadlock was eventually resolved by arbitration, the arbitrator upholding the decision of the board. This conflict is not merely an ironic comment on the prosperity which Co-operation had brought to both groups of workers. It is also a warning against taking the Principle of Equity and the considerations which derive from it too much for granted, and against neglect of that education and re-education in Co-operative Principles which every branch of the Movement should provide for its members.

In Co-operative Movements of agricultural producers, the supply societies, it has already been remarked, usually charge their members prices only slightly above the manufacturers' or wholesalers' prices rather than accumulate a surplus for ultimate distribution as dividend on purchases. In the marketing societies the Principle of Equity obviously requires that the distribution of profits shall be based on the amounts of produce the members offer their societies for sale or processing or both. The quality of the produce must also be taken into account, however, because quality influences prices. Where an organised market exists, a system of produce grading inevitably grows up and may even be enforced by some form of regulation, either adopted by the market itself or imposed by the State. A Co-operative marketing society, therefore, in order to obtain the maximum price advantage, must persuade its members to accept the grading system and agree to be paid according to the grade of produce and not simply the quantity they deliver to the society. For example, in a coffee-growing region, the payments made by a marketing society to coffee-growing members will vary according to how much arabica and how much robusta they deliver and the relative values of the two varieties of coffee bean on the market. For a wide range of products, the producers' Co-operative, especially if it engages in processing, extracts the most valuable element from the raw material it receives in its natural state; the only equitable method is thus to test each member's produce by sampling as well as weighing it, as soon as it is delivered. Hence a dairying society manufacturing butter tests its members' milk deliveries for their fat content and the resulting figures are a factor in calculating payments. Similarly, in a winemaking society with modern equipment, each member's grapes are weighed on delivery, immediately crushed and the juices tested for sugar content which determines the strength of the alcohol in the wine eventually made.

In both these cases and in numerous others the society is able to dispose of the 'waste' products, the skim-milk or the marc, either by sale in bulk or by subsidiary processing or by returning them to the members for use on their own farms. These economies, plus the price of the main product, constitute a more equitable return for their production than they are usually able to obtain from private dealers. One of the great advantages of the system of Co-operative slaughter-houses established in Denmark since the 1880's springs from the fact that their operations are on so large a scale that, in addition to curing and marketing the bacon (their main product), they are able to make and sell large quantities of pork products besides such non-edible articles as hides, bristles and blood and bone fertiliser, the revenue from which increases the disposable surplus applied to the benefit of the societies and their members.

Another way in which Co-operative marketing enables the producer to secure more equitable prices is by regulating the flow of products to market. It thus tends to minimise the downswing in prices which is inevitable when the whole of a crop is offered at or about the same time. The pressure on the market of small producers, anxious to obtain some ready cash and repay their most urgent debts, always offers opportunities to the dealer to buy cheaply in order to hold what he buys for a rise in prices later in the crop year when supplies are running down. The most celebrated example of the Co-operative method are probably those given by the 'pools', the marketing agencies of the Canadian wheat-growers. The grower receives a down payment on delivering his crop to his local elevator. This is a portion of the price of the grade of wheat he delivers. In the course of the ensuing crop year, he will receive one or more interim payments, if the state of the market and the operation of the Pool warrant them, and a final payment after the crop-year closes, accounts are balanced and surplus ascertained. The real return to the grower, the true price of his crop, is the aggregate of the several payments. Apart from the advantages of spreading his income more evenly over the 12 months, this system yields him something close to the full product of his labour and enterprise at the prevailing price level.

Difficulties in achieving Equity are liable to arise in agricultural Co-operatives, probably more in the future than hitherto, from differences in the scale of farming operations among their members. These differences are often reflected in varying costs, both to the farmers and their Co-operatives. A large farmer may be able to collect the fertiliser or machinery he has purchased or deliver his produce to his society in his own vehicles, whereas the small farmer may have no choice but to rely on the society's transport for either purpose. In the one case there is a saving, in the other an expense to the society. Should this difference be reflected in the sums due to or from the society payable or receivable by these members? If prices are uniform to all members, may there not be a certain unfairness to the members who save the society expense? Under present-day competitive conditions when attention is focused chiefly on prices and Co-operative societies are obliged to offer their members every inducement to reject attractive offers from private trade and loyally keep their business in Co-operative channels, the old solidarity which led the wealthier to make common cause with the poorer farmers is difficult, even impossible, to maintain beyond a certain point. A society with a mixed membership of large and small producers may not be able to contemplate the loss of volume it would suffer if the larger producers withdrew; the management will therefore be inclined to make concessions to retain their support.

Strict uniformity and equality of prices and treatment in other ways may not necessarily be equitable. In fact, in the agricultural Co-operative Movement it is frequently necessary to extend the consideration of Equity to what a society demands from its members, notably in regard to capitalisation. The shareholdings of individual members of agricultural marketing societies, for example, may be based on the area of land under a given crop or the number of cows or other livestock for which they need the services of the society. In housing Co-operatives again the member's deposits of capital are often required to be proportional to the value of the dwelling he wishes to acquire. Many credit societies relate the amount of credit they extend to members to the amount of members' deposits, share or loan capital.

Consumer Co-operatives have also had the need (or the expediency) of a similar refinement in adjusting prices to costs forced on their attention as retail trading margins have grown narrower. Supplementary services, such as home delivery, formerly included in the prices of goods, are being more and more abandoned. If prices are uniform, then it seems equitable to impose a special charge on those members who require goods delivered to their homes, in order to meet special costs not incurred for those who do not ask for this service. In the reverse direction, experiments have been made by offering price reductions to members who buy their requirements in bulk and carry them home in their own vehicles.

The justification for discussing these apparently minor aspects of the application of the Principle of Equity is that, as both managements and members grow more economically-minded, these questions will play a role of increasing importance in Co-operative business, whether that be retailing or agricultural marketing or supply. The achievement and maintenance of success in business may well depend upon their satisfactory solution — satisfactory that is to members as a whole. It must be borne in mind that the factors which have to be taken into account in distributing equitably the economic benefits of any Co-operative are to a high degree interdependent. Overall net profit depends on the relation between turnover and costs. In the latter, wages and salaries usually constitute the principal element and they, in turn, depend on the state of the market for the kinds of ability and skill which the Co-operative employs. Revenue from sales is also affected by the price policy — whether it is an active or a passive following of market movements — and the extent to which a system of cash discounts or rebates is practised. The disposable surplus may on the other hand be swollen by income from investments and dividends on purchases from Co-operative wholesale federations. Involved in every type of Co-operative are the specific interests of those who create the society and bear the final responsibility of entrepreneurs, those who supply the capital for its operations and the personnel of various grades it employs. The Principle of Equity requires that substantial justice shall be done to all of these interests.

CHAPTER SIX

Liberty

Liberty, as a Principle of Co-operation, is here considered in two main aspects. The first is the Liberty of the individual men and women who become members of Co-operatives; not only their freedom to join or leave them at will, but also their freedom of thought and action while they are members. The second is the Liberty of Co-operative institutions within the structure of society as a whole and also within the framework of the national and international Co-operative Movements of which they form part. The connection between the two aspects is implicit in the blunt affirmation made and endorsed by successive authorities of the International Co-operative Alliance between 1949 and 1951, as follows: 'In countries where the right of free association is denied and where any divergent opinions are suppressed, free and independent Co-operative organisations cannot exist'. Obviously it is not civil liberty in the broad sense which is the subject of this chapter nor yet the freedom of Association which is the external precondition of a genuine Co-operative Movement, but the freedom, individual and collective, required by Co-operative organisations as an essential condition of their functioning effectively.

This means that our discussion of Liberty must be related to what we have already observed of the operation of the other Co-operative Principles. Freedom is always relative to some kind of order of which it is, in a sense, a product. In the absence of any effective principle of order there can only be social chaos, characterised by licence for a few and oppression for the rest. Different social orders vary, of course, in the scope they allow for Liberty. In Co-operative forms of social organisation, the Principle of order, for reasons already stated, is necessarily Democracy. Since only those who are individually free are capable of taking collective decisions, Co-operative Democracy, in order that it may be vital and dynamic, demands freedom as its condition and complement. The claim of freedom to recognition as a Principle of Co-operation is therefore established.

If we accept this, we are in consequence bound to reject any suggestion that Liberty became recognised as a Co-operative Principle merely through the historical coincidence that the Co-operative Movement originated in Europe in a period when freedom of enterprise was the reigning economic orthodoxy. Undoubtedly, freedom of enterprise in the 19th century left the working population in industry and agriculture at liberty to listen to the message of a Schulze-Delitzsch, Raiffeisen or Charles Gide and to act upon it. In this way groups of people all over Europe had recourse to self-help in the form of free associations and, without expecting from the State anything more than the legal protection it was ready to grant to any honest form of enterprise, acquired economic power which enabled them to add to their widening political liberties a measure of economic freedom and independence hitherto beyond their grasp.

Notwithstanding the numbers of government-promoted and directed Co-operative organisations which have spread over the world in the last half-century, few if any of them have given evidence of the same vigour, stability and self-reliance which were displayed after 20 or 30 years' growth by organisations founded entirely on self-help when the State's attitude might be at best one of tolerance, but was often one of indifference or even suspicion. It is probably true that men and women who are accustomed to Liberty in society at large are the best able to accept and apply it when building and working Co-operative institutions. Nevertheless it is not in the circumstances of any particular continent or period of history, but rather in the nature of Co-operation iteself, that the justification for numbering Liberty among the Co-operative Principles is to be found.

Dr William King declared, as self-evident truth, that 'Co-operation is a voluntary act and all the power in the world cannot make it compulsory'. This statement may perhaps be described, not unfairly, as a rhetorical over-simplification. Not a single act, but consistent voluntary action implying countless acts and decisions directed over an unlimited period to consciously-accepted common ends, is what successful Co-operation demands of its participants. The personal involvement implicit by the term membership — expressed in the unswerving loyalty of many Co-operators to their societies — can only result from the engagement of their will. In 1947, when the newly re-constituted consumers' Co-operative in Hanover in Germany had only one small shop, members walked miles across the war-blasted city to make their purchases from it.

It is because Co-operatives, especially in their initial stages of development, depend on this resolute will on the part of their members that they normally do not ask that any one should be under the least compulsion to join them or stay with them longer than he or she desires. In either of these cases the will which the Co-operative needs is lacking. The passive, indifferent or reluctant member is a drag and an eventual source of disunity and economic weakness. This applies also to cases where a kind of indirect compulsion is exercised by the action of government when it channels essential supplies through Co-operatives in preference to less reliable types of enterprise. There may be cogent reasons of public policy for doing so under emergency conditions, but the result is almost invariably to weaken the Co-operatives through the adhesion of members or customers who use them to obtain articles unobtainable elsewhere and who cease to purchase or who desert them as soon as the shortage comes to an end. Of the hundreds of consumer Co-operatives started in India and other countries in the latter years of the Second World War, the majority were moribund, if not already in dissolution, five years after the fighting ceased. A similar kind of indirect compulsion accounts for the high figures of Co-operative membership reported by East European countries where Co-operatives form a permanent feature of centrally-planned and directed economies. The main difference is that the Co-operatives are not allowed to collapse through their inherent inefficiency, but are kept alive by a kind of artificial respiration provided by the propaganda of the ruling totalitarian party, as well as supported, directly, by their privileged position in the distribution of a wide range of commodities, and indirectly by the restrictions and disabilities imposed on other forms of trade.

Rather different is the compulsion sometimes advocated and occasionally enforced in the field of agricultural marketing. Where efforts to secure the orderly marketing of a product through voluntary Co-operatives have proved unsuccessful, largely owing to the individualism of the farmers, reinforced by the competition of private enterprises which offer better prices in order to check the expansion of the Co-operative, legislation has been invoked to require all producers to market their output through the Co-operative. Shortly after the First World War this method was adopted in some of the States of Australia. Similar attempts a little later in Canada to establish the compulsory pooling of wheat were unsuccessful. Whatever may be urged in its favour on grounds of public policy or on grounds of economy and equity, compulsory use of a Co-operative, although it may fall short of compulsory membership, is an infringement of Liberty. Like the trade unionists' 'closed shop', it achieves by the use of power what should be the end of a process of education. This amalgam of the functions of a Co-operative with those of a marketing board is different from the case of the 'binding rule' or contract system in agricultural marketing Co-operatives which is considered later in this chapter.

Constraint becomes practically unavoidable, however, in many newly-developed countries because of the time required by educational processes, especially among illiterate people. Under schemes of land-reform, when great estates are broken down among hitherto landless cultivators or tribal lands are divided among individuals, provision must be made for Co-operative credit, supply, processing and marketing, if the new owners are to develop their properties, make a decent living and repay mortgage loans. Co-operative membership and use of Co-operative services may thus become conditions imposed on those intending to benefit by the scheme. In a Malaysian project for jungle-clearance and rice cultivation visited by the author in 1958, the government had promised to support the cultivators until they made their holdings fully productive, but they on their side were obliged to deliver their rice for hulling and marketing to the local Co-operative. Such breaches of normal Co-operative liberty can perhaps be defended or tolerated if constraint does not become permanent but is acknowledged to be imposed for a limited period within which the member had a fair chance, not only to achieve economic independence, but also to gain experience and education in Co-operation.

It remains to be noted that the application of the rule of voluntary membership is normally modified in practice by other rules, based on common sense or sound business methods, intended to protect the interests of a Co-operative society as a whole. Thus, entry to a Co-operative may be practically automatic on the completion and signature of an application form. Such an application is rarely, if ever, challenged. Yet the society's rules usually provide for the approval of applications by the board of management, as well as for the right of the general meeting to reject an application which is successfully challenged by any member. The right of a society to protect itself against bad characters is no real restriction of the liberty of the great majority of decent members. Of greater practical importance are provisions in the rules against sudden resignations from membership, especially where the withdrawal of considerable sums of share capital may be financially embarrassing to a society. The rules usually entitle the management to insist on a period of notice before capital is withdrawn or they may provide for a period within which a member who has resigned may still be liable for a share of the society's debts. In the larger consumers' societies of Europe, however, it is remarkable how easily and speedily members are permitted to withdraw their savings, whether share capital or deposits, in the event of a death or other family emergency.

The concern of the Co-operative Movement for Liberty is further illustrated by the care taken to ensure that the liberties of individuals and of organisations are not restricted unnecessarily, but only so far as the needs of the common enterprise require. This is the explanation and justification of the so-called neutrality of Co-operative institutions in politics and religion. The aim of any Co-operative being to promote its members' economy, all that it requires of them when they join it is that they shall agree to be bound by its rules. This is the only provision which can possibly be regarded as a restriction of their personal freedom and even here all members have equal rights in amending or deleting rules which they find irksome, ineffective or old-fashioned. Members are not obliged to subscribe to any particular doctrine, whether religious, political or social, nor to accept any principles which are not inherent in the practice of Co-operation itself. No one's freedom of thought or opinion is compromised by membership of a Co-operative — indeed rather the reverse, for if a society is successful in reinforcing its members' economic power and independence, it often encourages them to greater boldness and freedom of expression in general.

The empirical grounds for adopting a policy of neutrality or independence of political and religious entanglements are easily understood. Political and religious doctrines are the matters on which people are most likely to disagree. To identify Co-operation with any particular doctrine is not merely to compromise the liberty of members by committing them to something with which they do not agree, but also to infringe the Principle of Unity by risking division among the membership and, at that, on a matter not essential to the achievement of their society's economic objectives. Obviously the term neutrality is ambiguous and for that reason has been in a great measure replaced by 'independence' among later generations of Co-operators. Neutrality does not mean and never has meant passivity or non-resistance where the interests of the Co-operative Movement or any of its branches are threatened or even involved. At the most, it can mean neutrality in relation to political parties but, even here, much depends on the attitude to Co-operation of the parties themselves. The more the State departs from laisser faire and assumes general responsibility for economic progress and social welfare, the more will it become involved with the Co-operative Movement and the Movement with it.

The Movement therefore cannot avoid the necessity of taking up attitudes, of expressing opinions and of initiating action on questions which are essentially — sometimes largely — political, affecting its members' economic interests. All depends upon its approach to them. If its attitudes and the policies it favours are truly grounded in Co-operative Principles and rightly designed to further the effective performance of its economic and social functions, they will be likely in the long run to strengthen rather than weaken its unity and, with that, its influences in the wider economic and social world. This can be achieved without giving any considerable body of members cause to complain of an infringement of their freedom of opinion or its opponents pretexts for denouncing alleged perversions of its true nature and objects.

The history of some of the European Co-operative Movements has important lessons to teach on the difficulties and disabilities which too close an attachment to political and religious doctrines imposes on Co-operative Movements in the discharge of their economic functions. Division along political and religious lines still results in a dispersion of Co-operative energies and resources — for example in Italy and, in regard to consumers' Co-operation especially, in Belgium. The effect of division is not merely to split the Movement into relatively small sections but also to diminish its aggregate size. In Holland the consumers' Co-operative Movement to a large extent reconciled its differences and united in a single overall federation, but the process of unification required more than a generation and the Movement served a smaller part of the retail market and exercised less powerful influence than it might have done if it had reached unity sooner. The leadership of the consumers' Co-operative Movement in West Germany was wise to recognise, when the Movement came to be reconstituted after the collapse of the Nazi regime, that the consumer is not a political category and that to perpetuate the former division of the Co-operative Movement into two wings with differing political and religious attachments would be foolish.

So far, this discussion has proceeded without touching upon the deeper connection between Co-operation and Liberty because this is to be sought more in the minds and behaviour of Co-operators themselves than in societies' rule-books. If, however, we are to discuss fruitfully the freedom of Co-operative organisations in relation to the Movement as a whole, we are bound to consider it, first of all, in relation to the individual member. Agreement to accept the rules of a society and conform to them does not measure the full extent of a member's obligation to his or her society. That can only be discharged if the member exerts what we have called a resolute will to support it. If members choose Co-operation for the sake of the advantages it promises, they will never reap those advantages unless they fulfil the conditions under which alone they can be realised. They must be willing to make the efforts and sacrifices, to pay the price, demanded for what they wish to enjoy. The freedom from exploitation which Co-operation promises can never be freedom in the familiar English phrase — to have one's cake and eat it. The members of a Co-operative cannot in the long run practise both Co-operation and individualism, either simultaneously or alternatively, as many unenlightened Co-operators seem to think. If they try to do so, their Co-operative will fail to yield its expected benefits, because its unity will be weakened and its bargaining power, as either buyer or seller, diminished. The shoppers who are lured away by the countless catch-penny inducements offered by competitive private trade from regular purchasing at a Co-operative store, or the farmers who succumb to the temptation to sell their produce to a dealer offering temporarily higher prices than their marketing Co-operative (often with the object of putting the Co-operative out of business), may in fact obtain short run advantages, but these are unlikely to exceed the long-term advantages they would derive from a Co-operative capable at all times of exerting its maximum power.

Of course individuals are often not so free as they fondly believe. The housewife may be free to enter as she pleases a Co-operative store, company supermarket or private shop, but what does that freedom signify if she is a brand-addicted victim of the 'hidden-persuaders'; if her choice of commodities is determined, not by the independent knowledge and judgement of their merits, but by the cumulative effect of newspaper, poster and television advertising and the example of neighbours as herd-minded as herself? Many consumers today are docile subjects of some millionaire's economic empire, transferable along with the assets and liabilities to some other concern according to the highest takeover bid. In the underdeveloped regions of the world, millions of agricultural producers live in debt-servitude to the village trader-cum-moneylender because, unless and until they practise Co-operation effectively, they are unable to do without him. Multitudes can never achieve, as individuals, economic independence and freedom from exploitation, but they can attain collectively an increasing measure of such freedom and independence through Co-operation — provided that they are willing to give up the largely illusory freedom of acting by themselves for the limited and conditional, but real, freedom they share on equal terms with their fellows.

It is important for the purposes of the present discussion that freedom shall be defined in positive no less than in negative terms (freedom **to** as well as freedom **from**), because that implies more than the mere absence of external restraint or constraint. Freedom is a product of the power which Co-operation generates. Because it confers power on those who practise it, Co-operation enlarges their freedom. It does not simply liberate consumers or producers from debt, it also enables them to spend or save or invest their money to the best advantage as they conceive it. Co-operation may also enable them to emancipate themselves from dependence on local markets or sources of supply and to sell their products or make their purchases in whatever market offers the most favourable prices and conditions. The more Co-operatives are able to dominate their economic environment, the more widely they extend their members' freedom to command all kinds of economic operations instead of remaining subservient to them. Moreover, the growth of the Co-operative Movement through successive applications of the Principle of Association, as described in Chapter Two, holds out the promise of indefinite enlargement of this freedom, provided that Co-operators themselves are able and willing to accept and fulfil the conditions. The progress of Co-operation, in short, demands at every important stage the surrender of lesser for larger liberties.

If there be any force in this reasoning, it should be possible to treat as more apparent than real any restriction resulting from the binding rule which obliges members of many agricultural marketing and processing Co-operatives to deliver the whole of their output of specified products (save the small quantities required for their own use at home or on the farm) to their society for disposal. This requirement, introduced in the early days of Danish Co-operative dairying and widely adopted in Scandinavia, is intended to give the society command of the largest and most regular volume of supplies possible, in order that it may run its processing plant economically and secure the best terms from the market. The rule is therefore a buttress of the economic power of the Co-operative and consequently of the wider freedom it confers on its members.

Is the binding rule, however, in a serious sense a restriction of Liberty? Hardly, because it can be adopted at the formation of any society, or later, only with the consent of the members as a body; and new members joining of their own accord, when the rule is already in force, should be aware of it as one of the conditions of their membership. It has also been pertinently observed that with the passage of time the rule has declined in importance, on the one hand because with improved education and understanding among the members of their obligations, it becomes less and less necessary as a support for efficient marketing; and, on the other hand, because the courts of law have been very reluctant, when Co-operatives have sought to enforce the rule in extreme cases on disloyal members, to concede their case, for one reason because of the indefinite duration of the obligation. If agricultural societies in a fiercely competitive situation resort to a 'contract' system to ensure regularity of supplies in their members' own interests, hardly anyone would contend that their members, by entering into a contract with their society, suffer any real loss of liberty, especially when the only other practical alternative is a contract, probably less to their advantage with a private firm.

The most difficult and complex problems encountered today in the application of the Principle of Liberty in the national Co-operative Movements arise within unions or federations of Co-operatives from the need to adjust the Movement's whole structure to the contemporary evolution of the general economic system. The federation of Co-operatives, as an application of the Principle of Association, has already been discussed in Chapter Two. Allusion was there made to the fact that federations are normally formed by primary Co-operatives in order to provide services which meet their common needs. Where a so-called Co-operative Movement is being promoted from the top downwards, a 'Co-operative union' may be created on paper by decree before any primary Co-operatives exist to be united, as in 1945 in the Soviet Occupation Zone of Germany. To such and similar cases, of course, the following remarks do not apply.

It is highly exceptional for the primary Co-operatives, which are all separate, self-determining legal entities, to surrender in principle any of their rights or liberties to the federations, except when they have clearly mismanaged their affairs and stand in need of rescue and rehabilitation. In time, the unions or federations usually come to exercise considerable influence over the primaries (the use of this term implies a kind of paternal relation) and the more the primaries depend upon them, the more this influence may verge upon domination, more especially in the trading federations than in the non-trading unions. The authority which even the oldest of the great national Co-operative unions exercise over their affiliates still remains today much more moral than constitutional or legal. The sanction of expulsion for societies persistently failing to support or actively opposing their Co-operative union on a vital point of policy is invoked only very rarely after all efforts at reconciliation or compromise have failed. A paradoxical situation can and sometimes does result when resolutions of the national congress, the Co-operative union's supreme authority, may remain largely inoperative because their implementation depends on action by the primary societies. The resolutions are binding upon the union's elected officers and salaried staffs, but not upon the societies whose delegates have voted and whose officers are responsible to their own general meetings.

One historic example was the fate of the recommendation made by the Independent Commission of Inquiry set up by the British Co-operative Union that the number of separate primary consumers' societies should be reduced by amalgamation to the extent of a few hundred. This recommendation (unlike some others) was adopted by the Congress, and the Secretariat of the Co-operative Union was charged with the task of preparing a plan on a national scale. A plan for reorganising the retail distributive structure of the Movement on the basis of 300 district societies was in due course drawn up, submitted and approved by Congress. It then became the duty of the Co-operative Union's Sectional (i.e. regional) Boards, assisted by the Secretariat, to implement the plan. The scheme was never fully realised but was overtaken by the course of events. It was followed by Regional Plans 1 and 2, but on the whole the amalgamation of British consumer Co-operatives continues according to no truly consistent plan.

A rather exceptional development resulted from the requirement of the Co-operative legislation of some countries, notably Germany and Austria, that primary Co-operatives shall be affiliated to unions invested with authority to audit their accounts. This is really compulsory federation, for it is indispensable to a society's legal existence, registration being refused by the district courts if the society cannot state the name of the audit union willing to grant it affiliation. This system would be defended by the majority of German Co-operators who would argue that, without such a legal obligation, the accounts of many primary societies, particularly the many village societies of various kinds, would never be efficiently or punctually audited. This is an argument from expediency and it reflects upon the low standard of Co-operative education of the members and officers of these primaries. The enforcement by the external authority of government of functions which the business sense of Co-operators themselves should tell them are indispensable to good management, is contrary to the spirit of voluntary movement and an infringement of its democracy.

The strict doctrine, if a hard one, would appear to be that, although authority to audit may be conferred by the State, the responsibility for ensuring that there is an audit and that it is duly carried out must rest upon the members who, if they are negligent, rightly suffer any resultant losses. This is, of course, not a criticism of the audit unions, for they have proved their value over and over again as a means of ensuring the financial stability and improving the management of the primary societies. Their scrutiny of the accounts goes much deeper than the verification of their correctness. The auditors' report on societies' financial policies and the instruction given to societies' boards of directors and officials have tended towards reasonable uniformity in their business policies and have built up a body of practice not inaptly called 'union discipline', which is an important factor reinforcing the unity of the national Co-operative Movement. Here and there the knowledge of the situation of primary societies revealed by the auditors' reports, combined with the knowledge of the abilities of Co-operative officials, gained through Co-operative training schools and the officials' subsequent records, have enabled national unions (e.g. KK in Finland) to exercise a healthy influence on the appointment of managers in the primary societies and in time establish their right to be consulted before such appointments are finally decided. As the importance of first-class management becomes more widely recognised and societies grow increasingly dependent on the technical guidance of the unions, the more they are likely to admit union intervention of this kind.

Rules of the Swiss Consumers' Co-operative Union, VSK, adopted at a special general assembly at Berne in November 1964, are of interest as an illustration of the limitations on their freedom of action which the Union's affiliated societies were willing to accept under present-day conditions. The first clause of Article 8 declares clearly that the autonomy of the societies in regard to their internal organisation and administration is not affected by their affiliation to the Union. The second clause, however, makes reference to certain exceptions which include, besides decisions taken by the Union's general assembly which have obligatory force, the conditions laid down for admission to affiliation (including open membership, democratic administration, cash payments, political and religious neutrality, dividend on purchases but not division of accumulated reserves, no competition between affiliated societies, etc). There are other obligations too, such as purchase from the Union of goods offered on the same terms as competitors; audit by the Union's fiduciary service; subscription to the Union's journals on behalf of their members and officers; admission of a Union delegation to meetings of governing bodies for consultative purposes; consultation with the Union on the appointment (or dismissal) of managers; and information to the Union on projected investments. Article 52 also empowers the Union to intervene when a society is obviously unable to conduct its business competently or it obstinately disregards the Union's advice.

Union discipline, as the events of the last decade have shown in several national Co-operative Movements, has not always been strong enough of itself to bring about the rapid regrouping and structural changes urgently necessary in order to make head against increasingly formidable competition. The need to reconstruct the retail store network on the basis of regional rather than local Co-operatives was foreseen more or less simultaneously in Britain, France and Germany. The explanation of the societies' sluggish response to the warnings and appeals of national leaders may be seldom simple and clear, but it would seem that it is not so often external obstacles as internal inhibitions which prevent Co-operative Movements from rethinking their strategy and redeploying their forces in the manner which changed circumstances demands. The speed with which the private shopkeepers, with the support of wholesalers, combined in voluntary chains in the 1950's against the same threat of the great multiple and supermarket firms stands out in marked contrast.

The example of the Austrian consumers' Co-operative Movement and its consolidation in Coop Austria, a central organisation involved in all branches of the Movement's activity, is worthy of study in greater detail than the present work permits. The consumers' Co-operatives which were reconstituted after the country's liberation from Nazi rule were partly reorganised on a district instead of a local basis. In the succeeding 1950's and 60's, a policy of amalgamation, transferring them step by step to regional societies, was by general agreement deliberately pursued. When regionalisation, more or less complete, seemed inadequate to counter actual or threatening competition, the final step was taken and Coop Austria was constituted. Statistically, the Austrian consumer Co-operative Movement is one of the smaller European Movements with an aggregate membership now exceeding 800,000. The quality of its achievement, however, is remarkable. The constitution of Coop Austria very largely took over the system of local democracy and member relations maintained for many years past in the regional societies, with the result that the aggregate attendance at the series of local regional and national members meetings for 1985 amounted to 108,000 or approximately one member in eight.

When the Co-operative Movement's procedures for reaching and executing decisions are compared, to its disadvantage, with the dispatch and ruthlessness of the unified administrations of big profit-making concerns, its democracy is often blamed and the remedy proposed is frequently administrative centralisation, equivalent to a managerial revolution, rather than efforts to make democracy effective. On the other hand, some who resist the amalgamation of independent primary Co-operatives into larger units claim to be defending democracy. On closer examination it would seem that what both parties are miscalling 'democracy' is nothing of the kind, but oncedemocratic institutions decayed and abused by oligarchy and minority rule. The real ground of objection to structural change and far-reaching concentration is not the Democratic Principle but loss of position in and power over snug little empires built up by elected officers and permanent officials who are as jealous of their independence as any national State of its sovereignty. The inhibitions have causes which lie deeper than the faults of Democracy in the failure of Co-operative leaders to comprehend and apply other Principles. Democracy is bound to be defective if the importance of Unity as a dynamic factor is not appreciated. Education of all kinds is narrow or neglected and the meaning of Liberty in a Co-operative context almost completely misunderstood.

Much of people's thinking about Liberty is still distorted by the individualistic fallacy which has ruled most Western thought on the subject for the last three centuries. It leads us into conceiving man's liberty as freedom **from** rather than freedom **with** his fellows. Disregarding the role of fellowship and society in any truly human mode of living, it brings us scarcely nearer to the concept of a free society than the chaos resulting from unco-ordinated and uncorrelated specialisation. As the inevitable contest between individualism and interdependence sways first to this side and then to that, modern society is inherently unstable. Social stability, together with economic efficiency, equity in distribution and Liberty itself, can only be established if a concept of social order comes to prevail capable of convincing the consciences of individual men and women and therefore of determining their conduct. Co-operation, if it is to display its richest potentialities, demands a freely-accepted discipline for the achievement of common ends, themselves freely chosen. In Co-operation true freedom has its analogue in what we commonly call the free execution of a musician or other artist. The artist's freedom is achieved by training brain, nerves and muscles to respond to his intentions. He becomes free to realise his conceptions when he is no longer hindered by the inability of his organs to respond to his impulses, either separately or in co-ordination — separately because the willed movement of one member must not be impeded by the unwanted movements of others; in co-ordination because the movements of some members require the movement or proper positioning of others. To play a single musical note on the piano or violin is impossible without co-ordinated movements of the fingers, hand, forearm, upper arm and even the trunk. But if co-ordination is to be free and unfettered there must also be independence. The pianist has to train himself, not only to use each hand in entire independence, but also to use every finger independently of its neighbour — and what is more, leave the momentarily unused member completely passive and relaxed. Tension induces rigour which impedes freedom.

The analogy here implied between artistic and Co-operative procedures is valid if we can accept Co-operation as being fundamentally an art of social organisation. The fact that this art is practised by groups and even multitudes, rather than by individuals, makes no real difference. In all its various manifestations, from the local primary society through national federation to the International Co-operative Alliance, Co-operation demands Liberty in Unity. The Unity springs from an overriding common purpose which should animate the wills of its adherents and towards which all its diversified activities tend. To achieve its ends, the Co-operative Movement must devise and practise a division of group and individual functions and ensure that its various units and sections are properly articulated, making their several contributions with the minimum of mutual interference and friction and maximum economy of effort to the grand overall result. No division of functions can be fixed for all time; it must be flexible and remoulded whenever it is found to hinder rather than help the Movement's progress — a process marked by the combination of lesser in greater integers and the corresponding merger of lesser in greater Liberties.

CHAPTER SEVEN

Responsibility or Function

The discussion of Liberty in the preceding chapter terminated in the affirmation that in the Co-operative Movement and, for that matter, society at large, true freedom is to a greater or lesser degree tempered by the necessity of organisation and the effective performance of functions. That implies that the concept of Function is inherent in Co-operation and its importance, its indispensability even, is recognisable by its influence on the application of the other Principles as the planets of the solar system influence one another's orbits. It will be remembered that the existence of Neptune was discovered not by the telescope, but by the fact that its influence on the movement of other planets could not be explained in any other way. The fact that Function was not considered by either the ICA Principles Committee of the 1930's nor the ICA Principles Commission of the 1960's is no reason for not discussing it in the 1980's. Liberty cannot be rightly enjoyed or exercised without Responsibility, which must therefore be given its place among the Principles of Co-operation.

The sixth Principle is denoted by the alternative terms Responsibility or Function, because these terms stand for two distinct but complementary aspects of one concept. That which is Function when viewed from the standpoint of society is Responsibility when viewed from the standpoint of the individual. The traditional Co-operative watchword 'Each for all and all for each' signifies more than just community, or mutuality of interest. It implies not merely attitudes but action. In the classic account of the 'spirit' of

Co-operation given by Dr William King in No. 7 of his *Co-operator*, the moral basis of the individual Co-operator's responsibility is clearly indicated. 'When a man enters a Co-operative society, he enters upon a new relation with his fellow-men', wrote Dr King. Friendship and comradeship, in his view, should not remain on the plane of vaguely diffused sentiment nor left to grow by chance or accident. They became 'a paramount duty and obligation' which should be enforced by every sanction a Co-operative community could bring to bear. Human societies, Co-operative or other, if they are to live, survive and achieve their purpose, have no choice but to organise themselves or be organised. This means something more than merely economic division of labour, although that is, of course, included. The society forms out of its own substance — the men and women who compose its membership — special groups to render particular services, not for their own benefit alone, but for that of all other members, that is, for the well-being of the society as a whole. Any given service will illustrate the way in which 'all' take care of the interests of 'each' through enlisting 'each' to minister to the interests of 'all'. A Co-operative society serves its members by performing functions in their interests, but it cannot do so effectively or even at all unless they in turn faithfully fulfil their responsibilities towards it.

The men of Rochdale, when they inscribed in their 'Law First' the phrase 'to arrange the powers of production, distribution, education and government,' were naming the vital functions which would have to be discharged in their ideal community when they came to establish it. The functions would not be discharged simply in the community, but on the community's authority, in its name, for its purposes, not for the sake of individual profit, ambition or aggrandisement. The Pioneers did not share the unfounded optimism of those economists or moral philosophers of an earlier generation who taught that through some pre-ordained harmony, the interests of the community would be best served by the unrestricted pursuit of individual interests. Their experience as workers and consumers had taught them other lessons. They did not deny, nor would they diminish, a man's or woman's responsibility for himself or herself, otherwise they would not have been such ardent propagators of self-help; but they believed that a proper sense of Responsibility, when enlightened, would lead men and women to organise themselves for combined action to achieve collective well-being. There is no reason to think that the Pioneers would not apply, in the society they actually founded, the functionalism they intended to adopt in the community into which, they hoped, the society would grow.

The fundamental role of the functional idea in Co-operative economic and social organisation is more clearly seen if we contrast it with the non-Co-operative business world. Dr Georges Fauquet and many after him have distinguished the two elements which are combined in a Co-operative society: the association of persons and the enterprise which serves their common needs. In fact they are to be distinguished only by abstract thought; there is no necessary physical separation. They are united by the fact that the association of persons is the entrepreneur. The entrepreneur's functions, as we observed in the chapter on Democracy, inhere in it. So far as individuals in a Co-operative society exercise entrepreneurial authority or discharge entrepreneurial functions, they do so as elected officers, paid servants or agents of the association. The self-appointed and self-responsible entrepreneurs — characteristic of capitalistic economic organisation, whether an individual or a group and governed by what the social philosopher Thomas Carlyle called the 'cash nexus' or connection between entrepreneur and shareholder, or between employer and worker — are foreign to Co-operative Economy. The common saying that companies are associations of capital, while Co-operatives are associations of persons, is driving at the same point: not that there are no, or should not be, monetary relations in Co-operative economic organisation — there obviously are and must be — but the cash nexus is not the sole or principal bond between individuals or groups performing specialised functions. The vital bond is constituted by the concept of membership.

The language we employ in discussing these questions and the metaphors involved in the terms we use are significant and not to be ignored, for they point to deep and far-reaching resemblances. The people who join Co-operative societies and collectively assume responsibility for them are called members. They have relations with their societies as shareholders or customers because such functions as the contribution of capital, buying, selling, borrowing or depositing all spring from the fact that they are members, parts of one body. The word 'member', derived from the Latin word for a limb, cannot signify anything other than a part of a larger whole. The term carries implications of mutual dependence — of the whole body on the limb and of the limb on the whole body. The fable of Aesop, the moralist, of the belly and the members shows how deeply the idea of function is embedded in the wisdom of our ancestors. It also illustrates how liable specialists can be to form mistaken judgements, if their vision of the whole system they serve is not adequate to correct them! Similarly with the term 'organisation', which it is completely impossible to avoid using in this context. The word 'organ' in the original Greek denoted an instrument. By analogy it was applied to specialised parts of the body, e.g. the eye as the organ of sight, and thence transferred by a second analogy to human society. Just as the physical body breathes, nourishes itself and moves from place to place by adapting and locating particular sorts of cells to serve as constituents of organs, so the body social selects, trains and locates its members for specialised duties fulfilling its various purposes. It would be, of course, a mistake to press this analogy too far. The life of societies and physical organisms is by no means in every respect similar, but the association of life everywhere with organisation is a warning against too mechanistic a conception of Co-operative structures.

The fundamental role of organisation in modern society was probably first fully appreciated by Saint-Simon and his school. Saint-Simon himself brought out in 1819 a short-lived review which he called significantly *L'Organisateur*. His purpose was to induce his countrymen to direct their thinking more towards the social structure into which their nation was evolving than towards the past or present out of which it must evolve. Into the controversy which raged among French intellectuals 150 years ago, mainly between the liberals, who favoured political democracy and free competition in economics, and the traditionalists who harked back to the feudal and hierarchical regime prevailing before 1789, Saint-Simon injected a third element, the idea of constructing a new order. In his reading of history, feudal society, which had been dominated by the warrior in things temporal and the priest in things spiritual, had broken down into a transitional system dominated by jurists and metaphysicians; their tasks were largely destructive and they were preparing the way for a new order under which leadership would pass to the scientist and the industrial organiser.

Saint-Simon was obviously much more of an intuitive than a systematic thinker. It was his disciples, working upon his fragmentary ideas and suggestions, who later gave definition and coherence to those which had positive value. In particular, they sharpened the opposition between the social principle of antagonism (competition) and association. They rejected the individualism of classical economic theory and its corollary of free enterprise. They denied that the liberty and rights of the individual can serve as basis for any true social order. The constructive principle was rather association, spreading from the family to the community, from the community to the nation, and from the nation to the confederation of nations. This should be the animating spirit of the society of the future. In the economy of private enterprise the industrialist exploits the labour of the proletariat which, while nominally free, has no choice but to accept his conditions or starve.

This led the Saint-Simonians inevitably to advocate the abolition of private property in the instruments of production and the transfer of the right of inheritance from the individual to the State. The instruments of production being socially owned, they could be entrusted for industrial operations to approved associations of social groups directed by chosen functionaries. The Saint-Simonians were not democrats, for they associated democracy with the rule of lawyers and metaphysicians which was destined to pass away. On the other hand they strongly defended the claims of ability and merit against the privileges of wealth. Their social concept is one of a hierarchy in which individuals would be assigned places according to their various capacities and rewarded according to their performance. What is important for our present discussion, however, is that the Saint-Simonians set up, over against what the British economist, R. H. Tawney a century later called the 'acquisitive society', a society based on the idea of Function — an idea common to all the Socialistic schools which have succeeded them, including Co-operation.

In so doing, the Saint-Simonians seem to have returned to an old, rather than to have discovered a new idea. It was an idea which appeared to have vanished, at least temporarily, from current thinking on social problems, in the last quarter of the 18th century, when the idea of society itself seemed to be eclipsed by all-conquering individualism and the cash nexus had achieved predominance among human relations. The liberal explosion, detonated by Rousseau's Social Contract and Adam Smith's exposition of 'the obvious and simple system of natural liberty' (as he called it), and reverberating round Europe in the wars of the French Revolution and the spread of the Industrial Revolution from Great Britain to the Continent, may well have been necessary and in the end inevitable, because the crumbling ruins of feudalism had outstayed their time and were blocking the advance of mankind into a new age.

The rise and decline of feudalism occupied a thousand years of European history and, in the corrupt and oppressive institutions which the French and succeeding revolutions abolished, it was scarcely possible to distinguish any more the fundamental principles which inspired it. Although their application was never anywhere or at any time uniform, these principles gave feudal society order and cohesion. In the feudal system, individuals, communities and 'estates' were held together by mutual obligations of loyalty, service and protection. The villeins who cultivated the soil were not slaves. In return for the services they rendered to the lord of the manor, the villein and his fellows had their rights against the lord, and the lord, if he could command their obedience in many things, had duties to fulfil towards them. Often much depended on the existence of a strong central government and its power to ensure that statute law and manorial custom were respected, but the position of the villein was diametrically opposite to that of the mid-19th century proletarian. The latter, if theoretically free to work whenever he could find employment, had no general right to work or claim to a living and was excluded from the parliamentary franchise if he owned no fixed property. The proletarian lived by the purchasing power of his wages and when wages ceased and his meagre savings were exhausted, he and his family starved, even in the midst of abundance. If the villein starved, it was because the whole manor starved together through failure of its crops or the ravages of war or the plague.

The feudal system was eroded by the development of markets and the increasing use of money to commute services. Still more was the system corrupted by the separation of duties from rights, for the rich and powerful could find ways of enforcing their rights while exempting themselves from their duties, whereas the poor and weak could offer little resistance when their duties and levies were increased or their rights were rendered null and void. But rights not justified by corresponding duties become mere privileges and duties enforced on those without rights become servitude. Such an affront to natural justice was doomed to destruction in the name of Liberty, Equality and Fraternity. Unfortunately, revolution when it came left little standing between the State with its sovereignty, on the one hand, and the individual with his rights on the other. And Association was one of the rights which he was denied for a generation or longer. It was left for the Saint-Simonians to dig out Association from the debris of the Revolution and set it once more on its rightful pedestal and, with it, the idea of Function.

The Saint-Simonians, however, remained a small, obscure and somewhat eccentric sect whose immediate influence on public opinion and the general course of events was very slight indeed. The idea of Function therefore remained in eclipse for some time. Its reappearance and rehabilitation resulted from the impossibility, as modern industrial society evolved, of doing without it. Meanwhile, irresponsibility reigned in the private and capitalist sectors of economic life and even today the nature of Responsibility can often be illustrated more clearly from its breach than from its observance.

Dominant in social evolution since the beginning of the 19th century has been the unending succession of new scientific discoveries and technical innovations which open prospects of enrichment to the capitalist entrepreneur. He finds his justification in orthodox economic doctrine, even though that is not so involved as it once was with the fiction of economic man and the individualistic fallacy. Since the advent to power of the bourgeoisie, the claims of wealth upon society have become no less onerous than the claims of birth which they superseded, while the duties acknowledged by or demanded of wealth were, certainly at first, too few and too tenderly enforced, lest 'enterprise' (a gloss upon acquisitiveness) be discouraged. From the middle of the 19th century, however, the pendulum began to swing slowly back. The emergence of working-class movements, more or less inspired by socialistic ideas, and the awakening of the social conscience, shocked by the sub-human living and working conditions imposed upon wage-earners, combined to compel governments to impose more and more responsibility upon entrepreneurs for the health, safety and general well-being of their workers. With the passage of time also, a new type of entrepreneur appeared in the form of Co-operatives, formed by consumers and producers to defend themselves against exploitation; municipalities, organising services in the public interest; and the State, desirous of keeping natural or technical monopolies under social control.

Nevertheless the evolution of private and capitalist economic organisation proceeded generally on lines which the Saint-Simonians had forecast. The economic system's insatiable appetite for capital obliged entrepreneurs to resort to Association through the company form of organisation which came in the end to dominate the whole scene. As the typical enterprise grew in scale its governing structure inevitably tended to become hierarchical and, as companies amalgamated or combined in other ways to form cartels, trusts and widely-ramifying concerns, these hierarchies became increasingly self-maintaining, remote and in practice exempt from the control of the shareholders to whom they were nominally answerable, and still more of the community at large or of government as its representative. Relations became mostly impersonal. There was and is normally no moral or social bond between company and shareholders whose interests are purely monetary. Attracted in the first place by prospects of gain in the form of income from company profits or the appreciation of capital values, the latter can at any time sell their shares and invest the proceeds elsewhere, if the prospects appear better. Anonymous and fluctuating in its composition, the typical company is not a body capable of either exacting or bearing social Responsibility.

So far as the employees of companies are concerned, although public authorities may be able to enforce Responsibilities on companies **for** their workers, they cannot impose responsibility **to** them. Irresponsible enterprise inevitably gave rise to irresponsible trade unionism, for the workers would neither feel nor shoulder Responsibility for a system which demanded obedience from them while denying them a voice in policy or administration. If labour be treated simply as a commodity, then the workers' interest is limited to their bargaining power and what it can secure for them in the shape of rising wages, the security of their jobs, the comfort and safety of their working environment and the extension of their leisure. Nor does irresponsibility necessarily diminish with the improvement of working conditions and living standards, if there is a simultaneous weakening of trade union discipline. Workers no less than employers can yield to the temptation to abuse power even against the advice and warnings of their union officials. The advent of full-time employment and the so-called Welfare State were accompanied in more than one country by an inclination to down tools without notice on trivial pretexts, to attempt to predetermine the results of negotiation by resort to strike action or the threat of it, and to exploit key positions in industrial organisations in order to extort favourable terms, regardless of the damage and loss inflicted on the industry or the community by refusing to work or negotiate. Nor is there any reason to believe that the immense majority of wage-earners are anything but content with a system under which they can at once repudiate Responsibility and increase their income.

The foregoing statement has been, for the sake of brevity, over-simplified. It is not contended that no sense of social Responsibility exists among entrepreneurs or workers of various grades. As a rule there is Responsibility enough to ensure the fulfilment of contracts, agreements and undertakings; without moral standards generally observed, the economic system would collapse. The point is rather that where obligation stems, not from status, but from contracts, the terms of which are settled by superiority in bargaining power, and in which the main motive is commercial profit, gain by investment or, at least, the avoidance of financial loss, social obligation is liable to be thrust into second place or even lower in the scale of values. It is not denied that there have been many examples of entrepreneurs capable of rising above self-interest and keeping constantly aware of the services they and their undertakings should render to the community, just as there have always been workers by hand or brain whose sense of solidarity and obligation reached far beyond their fellow-trade unionists, their occupation or the working classes in the mass. But they are rather exceptional than typical. In a society in which the desire to make money is regarded as laudable ambition, and the possession of a large fortune a title to respect, people's minds are bound to be confused as to the purpose of economic activity in relation to social well-being and to regard it as an end rather than a means.

This confusion exists notwithstanding the gradual but irresistible abandonment of laisser faire over the last century. In contemporary mixed economies there is continual tension between the economic and the social, largely because social responsibilities have had to be imposed on industry and commerce from without. This is to be seen, for example, in the welfare legislation to which enterprise has to conform for the benefit of the workers; the company legislation which penalises promoters or administrators who defraud the public; the measures for protecting consumers against adulteration and other malpractices; and the constant attempts to prevent or break up socially dangerous concentrations of economic power. Yet the normal and natural evolution of the economic system, even under capitalist leadership, tends constantly in the direction of closer and more complex integration, not simply between similar or mutually complementary enterprises, but also between industry and industry (witness the growing dependence of agriculture on the chemical, machinery and petroleum industries) and between national economies (witness the attempts to establish common markets or free trade areas). The complexity of the resulting problems and the massive capital resources committed make accurate, long-term forecasting and planning indispensable and, with them, ever closer consultation and interdependence between business enterprise and governments. Under these conditions enterprise may become in some ways more responsible; it may equally acquire a more powerful influence over governments and their economic policies. It becomes ever more difficult to determine who governs whom. At least it may be confidently affirmed that the economic world has progressed considerably since the days when the right of individual or capitalist enterprise to initiate and direct economic enterprise for profit went unquestioned. The idea of Function haunts contemporary economy. Capitalists with a conscience seek to justify their activity and render homage to virtue by claiming that they are performing services for the community, even though they are working for profits. This, however, is not a functional system as a Co-operator would understand it, if only because the capitalist entrepreneur would not be accountable to the proper authority.

A model Co-operative functional structure was outlined in a masterly paper by Theo Braun, President of the French National Federation of Mutual Credit, presented to the Third International Conference on Co-operative Thrift and Credit held in London in 1974. Dealing with Structure, Co-ordination and Power, Braun took for granted that the basic units of a Co-operative system are autonomous. In them the four centres of Responsibility (and therefore power) are the membership, the elected administration, the management and the employees. The running of the Co-operative depends upon the proper functioning between these four elements and the relations between them. The danger to be guarded against is the shifting of the power of decision from the administration to the technicians. Much therefore depends on the ability and training of administrators.

The elected administrators are most likely to have received no training at all before their election and not much after it, but will have 'picked up' what they know and what skills they may ultimately develop by imitating their senior colleagues. The unanswered question most of the time is, who is to give training? And possibly also, who is to train the trainers? One of the advantages of the former German system of local and district committees was that there was always a reserve of partly-trained personnel graduating from shop and district committees to the supervisory council of the society on which to draw. But in Great Britain, where the attendance at meetings tends to diminish the larger the societies become, there is no such reserve and the calibre of the average committee person steadily declines.

This is the danger point described by Theo Braun, when the manager, who has had training, wants a decision from the elected administrators which they may refuse or at least hesitate to give. With less foresight than the manager, they may not be able to see the consequences of their decision or indecision. Either the manager leaves the matter undecided and the society suffers because of a decision not taken, or he may persuade the committee to leave the matter in his hands and in effect usurp the committee's functions, thus impairing the society's democracy. In many matters the elected committees must trust the appointed official. The object of training the committee is that it shall know when it should trust him and when it should trust its own judgement and be right each time.

There is no danger of a similar kind when the primary units are federated in a secondary organisation. A shift of undue power to the federation must be obviated by maintaining mutual confidence and helpfulness. The federal structure develops vertically by the establishment of a tertiary organisation, a confederation, whose function is to ensure the Movement's cohesion by defining its common objects and securing the right subsequent action, besides its representation before governmental and other external organisations. Within the confederation, the specialisation of functions creates social centres of responsibility each with its delegated powers, requiring constant efforts to strike a balance and come to terms with one another in order to maximise the efficiency and effectiveness of the whole.

Theo Braun maintained that Co-operative organisations demand such an 'institutional' framework, not a 'contractual' system with such devices as exchange of shareholdings and interlocking directorates as in the ordinary business world. In other words, in a Co-operative system the autonomous elements respect each other's powers and responsibilities and become inter-dependent through inter-Co-operation. Within the confederation there is a continual dialogue which reconciles differences and establishes a collective discipline based on a global conception of the whole. In such a structure the Principle of Function complements both Liberty and Democracy.

In the centrally planned and directed economies of totalitarian states under one-party rule, in theory at least, economic organisation and activity are recognised as social functions initiated and led by officers appointed by duly constituted authorities. But here the question may legitimately be posed, whether such a system is not a functionalism imposed upon the economic organisation in order to ensure its subservience to political ends, rather than a functionalism built into the economic organisation to make it responsive to social needs. But once again it would not correspond to the Co-operative idea of Function because it is in general not associated with Democracy, Equity or Liberty.

For the essence of Co-operation consists in membership of a free association and willing acceptance and discharge of the obligations, statutory and moral, which membership entails. So far as it has developed, it exemplifies the character of an economic system based on functionalism. The Principle of Function, like the six others, pervades the whole Co-operative structure. The meaning of Dr Fauquet's epithet *responsables et solidaires* is that each Co-operator, while answering for himself and his own welfare, is conscious of his trusteeship for the interest of his fellow-members. This trusteeship includes loyal support of the society's economic action and also faithful discharge of all the functions of membership, because it is under these conditions alone that the society can maximise its economic power and benefits. Conversely, disloyalty and neglect of a member's duties are breaches of trusteeship, as they tend to weaken the society and in the end to damage the interests, not of the disloyal alone, but of all the rest. Moreover, though a Co-operator may feel a sentiment of loyalty primarily to his society, his obligations do not end there. He and his fellow-members of the society owe a collective loyalty and have collective functions to discharge towards any federation to which their society affiliates and therefore on as far as Co-operative solidarity may extend — even to the very limits of the international Co-operative Movement. The Principle of Responsibility or Function is not one for office-bearers only. The rule of 'Each for all and all for each' signifies that Co-operators everywhere are responsible both for and to one another.

CHAPTER EIGHT

Education

Experientia docet (experience teaches) said the Romans. Life educates, said J. H. Pestalozzi, the great Swiss educationist, echoing them with a difference. Co-operation, as a part of life and experience, also educates in the same sense. This sense, however, is more restricted than at first appears. Experience teaches those, and only those, who are willing and able to learn from experience and only within the limits of their experience. Life educates, but it can equally miseducate through the force of bad examples and even render people, through privation, disillusionment and despair — perhaps also unexpected or undeserved prosperity — ineducable. Co-operation educates by making demands on its participants which they can meet only in so far as they are able to acquire fresh knowledge and adopt new modes of behaviour. This education can sometimes be very effective, although — possibly because — there may be no conscious effort to learn.

Nevertheless, while that may illustrate the close affinity of Co-operation with education, it is not what is meant when Education is discussed as a Co-operative Principle. Education is a Principle, an indispensable element in Co-operation, because it is essential to the existence of Co-operatives, to the understanding and practical application of the other Co-operative Principles, to the growth of Co-operative organisations and to the progress of the Co-operative Movement — a movement which must begin and continue in the minds of men and women. There can be no Co-operation without Co-operators and

Co-operators, unlike poets, are not born but made. Co-operation, therefore, cannot trust to unconscious education alone; it must consciously employ suitable kinds and methods of education as instruments to achieve its ends.

Since Co-operation implies not simply knowing but doing (and doing effectively), education for its purposes must be given a very wide denotation which includes much besides the ordinarily accepted types of academic instruction. In one sense, it is roughly equivalent to the sum-total of acts and experiences which promote the mental and moral growth of the individual Co-operator and the development of his or her capacity for working with others according to Co-operative Principles. Man's collective work, an eminent contemporary sociologist has observed, cannot rise above his personal scale of values. The progress of Co-operation cannot continue unless Co-operators are both resolved and able to attain ever higher standards of efficiency and morality. They have to be not simply educated for Co-operation; they have to be continuously re-educated in Co-operation. The Co-operative Movement cannot regard Education as any other than a life-long experience.

Co-operative Education must be given a wide definition for another reason, which is that in the final analysis all education is self-education. Learning, like Co-operation, is a form of self-help. There is force of course in the aphorism: He that is but self-taught has a fool for his master. But learning **for** oneself need not imply learning **by** oneself, any more than self-help in the economic sphere excludes mutual aid. It is important to recognise, however, for the purpose of Co-operative Education, that learning, whether to know or to do, precedes teaching and depends upon the unquenched appetite of the individual for knowledge and skill. Teaching is relevant or important only in so far as it may be the best method of promoting learning. The test of any system claiming to be educative is whether it provides experiences enabling the learner to develop his own powers and personality, and this is an added reason why the Co-operative Movement, in applying its Principle of Education, is bound to go beyond traditional academic education, which in its purposes and its methods is often totally unsuitable for the aims Co-operation has in view.

Does the definition of Co-operative Education include propaganda? If in theory 'no', in practice 'yes'. Much of Co-operative Education cannot help being propaganda; all Co-operative propaganda ought to be, to a considerable degree, educational. It is important, however, for Co-operators to understand the difference between education and propaganda so that they can easily tell one from the other, even when the two are presented in a compound or mixture. One obvious difference is that, whereas the educationist usually endeavours to influence the masses through his action on individuals, the propagandist will more often be found trying to influence individuals through his action on masses. On a deeper level, there is a vital difference of aim from which differences of method mostly arise. The aim of the propagandist is to persuade people to think, feel and act as he wishes, whether that be to accept the product he advertises as the best and to buy it, or to accept the political doctrine he advocates and vote for his party or candidate. If people do what he wants, his object is achieved, no matter if, next week or next year, he tries to persuade them to do just the opposite.

The educationist on the other hand, is not primarily interested in **what** the individual thinks or believes, but rather in **how** he thinks and reaches his opinions — that is, in his power to apprehend facts clearly and to reason from them to valid conclusions, and how that power to think for himself can be developed. In the practical sphere the educator is concerned with the individual's power to act, with his skill and performance in various directions, in order to develop them to the limits of his native ability, as means whereby he can serve the community and, maybe, express himself. Whereas the propagandist's aim may be a momentary act, such as making a cross on a ballot paper, the educationist's aim is to cultivate a talent or capacity which remains the individual's permanent possession. These distinctions are not absolute, but they indicate the necessity for Co-operators to be able to distinguish education from propaganda and to be clearly aware what they are doing when they employ either.

Finally, it must be observed that a place must be reserved in every system of Co-operative Education for the impartial, dispassionate pursuit of pure knowledge, undisturbed by any practical aims. From this realm, propaganda must be strictly excluded because of its unavoidable exaggerations, distortions and suppressions. The educated Co-operator must be capable of contemplating in cold blood the uncoloured truth — even about Co-operation.

The educated Co-operator, what sort of person is he or she? This question is not in any way idle or irrelevant. The proof of the effectiveness of a Co-operative or any other system of education lies in its power to set its stamp on the minds and personalities of those who pass through it. The social Principles of Co-operation, regarded on their reverse side, are principles of conduct for the individual Co-operator. The educated Co-operator will be distinguished by his competence in conducting Co-operative affairs according to Co-operative Principles, by his capacity to frame policies and build institutions which satisfy the demands of all the Principles in the manner best suited to the objects in view and the circumstances of the time, and by ability to work happily and successfully as a member of a team. These are his general characteristics, despite the infinite ways in which men and women can differ in intelligence, character and temperament. His Co-operative education must be a synthesis of the knowledge, technical training and social discipline required for the competent performance of his functions in the Co-operative Movement, whether as a member, elected officer or salaried servant in an executive or subordinate position.

The Principle of Education requires that the smallest and simplest of Co-operatives, no less than the biggest of Co-operative federations, shall constantly strive to increase its members' fund of knowledge and to perfect its working methods by whatever educational methods and agencies are available to it. New Co-operative societies, especially in the developing countries, may well first appear to their prospective members as education in the embryonic form of friendly discussions between neighbours on their common economic problems and difficulties, instigated perhaps by a field worker, versed in adult educational method, in the service of a government Co-operative department or a Co-operative union. The field worker's first aim is not to impart knowledge, for the requisite knowledge is all within the experience of the group, but to provoke discussion and unobtrusively to guide it along constructive channels towards practical attempts to solve common problems through joint action. At the point when the general consensus recognises that such action is possible and desirable, the field officer can begin to supply factual information about Co-operatives, leading on to theoretical knowledge of the Principles on which they work. Once action is decided upon, the discussion group evolves into a primary Co-operative, framing its rules, defining its objects, possibly accumulating capital, as the debate continues.

The Co-operative once formed and registered and its officers elected, the members will need training in the procedures of general meetings and the working methods of their society; the management committee members will require guidance in the performance of their duties; and whoever is appointed manager or secretary will probably also need instruction and supervision, at least at first. All will continue to learn, it may be hoped, as the society's work develops, and begin to distil some practical wisdom from their experience. The process here described, or something very like it, was followed with conspicuous success in the Co-operative pioneer work carried out some 50 years ago in the Maritime Provinces of Canada by the Extension Department of the St Francis Xavier University of Antigonish, Nova Scotia. Thanks to the training carried out by the University in social leadership through the Coady Institute, this system of Co-operative Education is spreading far and wide in the developing countries. Its great merit is that it exemplifies not merely education in Co-operation, but also Co-operation in education. Practice and theory are not divorced but united as aspects of one concept — Co-operation.

In the simple example just given of the role of Education in the formation of a primary Co-operative, it will be observed that the elements of knowledge, technical training and social discipline are already all three present. In old established

Co-operative Movements they may be seen in an advanced stage of development as a network of interlacing institutions. These may include adult educational courses, a popular and a technical Press, Co-operative training schools and colleges, departments for publicity and public relations, departments for film or video distribution and production and so forth, all established and operated, separately or in combination by Co-operative organisations of all types. By no means to be ignored is the Co-operative Education organised within the academic world in the form of school and student Co-operatives and the institutions for Co-operative studies and research established by a number of famous universities within their faculties of economics and sociology. The scope and structure of these various Co-operative institutions are bound to differ according to the circumstances of every country, the development of its system of public instruction and the policies of its educational authorities and organisations. In applying its Principle of Education, the Co-operative Movement is not obliged to provide every kind of education its members and officers require. Its responsibility is simply to ensure that Co-operators are educated in the ways, and to the degree, that their functions in the Movement demand for efficient performance.

This has meant, both in the past and today, that where national systems are underdeveloped and their deficiencies are not made good by other agencies, the Co-operative Movement has provided the education which its members or personnel lacked. As is well known, the Rochdale Pioneers in their early days helped their illiterate members to become literate and provided a lending library and reading room so that all members could continue their general education and keep reasonably well-informed on current events. Over the years, the Pioneers went even farther in the direction of Co-operation for education by arranging lectures and courses for adults in different branches of knowledge for which a need or an interest existed among the membership, thus helping to make good for working people, who normally left school at 14 years of age or earlier, the omission of the State system to provide systematic education for adults. In time, as other institutions such as the Workers' Educational Association and the extra-mural departments of universities staked their claims in this field and the State came to recognise its responsibility for aiding them, the Co-operatives took a less prominent part, while continuing to support, financially and in other ways, forms of adult education directly beneficial to the Movement. The relations between the Co-operative Movement and other educational agencies must remain fluid and flexible in a rapidly changing world, first in order that the Co-operative Movement can make the most effective and economical use of whatever resources it can devote to education, and second that it can contribute, more especially to the education of the citizen, that combination of thought and action, of the ideal and practical, of stability with progress, which is its outstanding merit.

There is always a close correspondence between the development of adult education in any country and the level of the performance of its Co-operative institutions. The classic example is, of course, Denmark where a system of adult education — the folk high schools or people's colleges — was in existence almost a generation before there was any large-scale Co-operative development, particularly among the rural population. There is no doubt at all that Denmark's rapid advance to the forefront of the agricultural Co-operative Movement is due to the liberal education received by young farmers in the people's colleges during the winter months. The close and friendly relations between the Co-operative Movement and the people's colleges did not obviate, however, the need for the Co-operative Movement in time to establish its own schools and courses for training in Co-operative and business techniques, as well as its own Press for keeping its members' knowledge up to date.

Among the most exemplary systems of Co-operative Education are those developed by the Swedish consumers' Co-operative Movement for employees and members during more than six decades. They owe much to the late Harald Elldin, the most original of Co-operative educators in this century, who was appointed head of the Department of Co-operative Studies of Kooperativa Förbundet, the Swedish Union-Wholesale, about 1920. Since space will not permit an adequate account here of his methods and ideas, it must suffice to say that he broke completely from traditional pedagogy and started afresh from a consideration of the geography and social life of Sweden, the working lives of the students he had to train and the kinds of service for which he had to make them competent. He rejected the lecture as a method of teaching as conducive to mental and physical torpor and substituted for it study in small graded groups in which the participants learned by gathering their own information from original sources, discovered every aspect of the subject studied, and worked out practical solutions to problems of modern retailing.

Sweden has a large territory with a relatively small population. In order to avoid excessive expense of travelling and long absences from the employees' daily work, Elldin based his instruction on correspondence courses, bringing students to the College only for periodic short interim study sessions. In time he was able to recruit assistants from the older students. These acted as advisers and guides to the study groups but also continued their studies of advanced technical problems. Only a few of them remained on the College staff; the rest mostly left for management positions in Kooperativa Förbundet or one of its affiliated societies. The learning system thus maintained a constant supply of competent workers, but it must also be said that it did not necessarily meet all the Movement's needs in personnel.

Discussion groups also formed the training skills of Co-operative member-education. They are numbered by thousands and their studies extend to subjects other than Co-operation. They are never left to flounder their own way along, but are provided with ready-made courses and expert advice and guidance by the staff specially trained in a department of the head office of the Co-operative Union. The groups not only receive help; they are expected to report the course and the conclusion of their discussions to the central office to be commented upon by the advisory staff. This remarkable combination of discussion groups with correspondence tuition results in a wide diffusion of sound Co-operative knowledge and opinion throughout the consumers' Co-operative Movement; it enables the leadership to take the pulse of the membership and to gain understanding and support in advance of major changes of policy. Special research has again and again been organised and text books written. It meets the particular need of the discussion groups. In the famous confrontation between Kooperativa Förbundet and the European electric lamp cartel, Anders Hedberg was commissioned to write a book on the role of the cartel in the electricity industry. The book was studied in the groups while KF's factory was being built and the whole market represented by the consumer Co-operative Movement was aware of what was at stake, ready to purchase the lamps before production began.

In a brief review of the 'content' of Co-operative Education — knowledge, technical training and social discipline — we may note first of all that the knowledge needed by Co-operators is systematic in varying degrees. All Co-operators need information, that is, up to date, accurate knowledge of facts and events bearing upon practical tasks and decisions to be reached or executed. All Co-operators need the technical knowledge which relates to the working of Co-operative institutions, particularly the Movement's democratic machinery. Beyond this are fields of knowledge which are extremely valuable without being always indispensable to efficient Co-operative practice, notably the history of the Movement's origins and development and past events which have determined its present situation. There is also the economic and sociological knowledge yielded by the scientific study of Co-operation as a social phenomenon among many others — knowledge which becomes increasingly systematic as research extends and criticism becomes more searching.

The constant aim of Education must be to create and maintain in the minds of Co-operators a many-sided awareness of the Movement and the manner in which it promotes their interests. This aim cannot be achieved unless information is conveyed to them in such a way that it is virtually impossible for them to ignore it. It must be taken to them; it is useless to expect them (or many of them) to seek it, especially in our contemporary society when such a multitude of interests and causes clamour for their attention. In many countries where the Movement is long-established, the membership is now so large as to be indistinguishable from the general public. The Movement is unable to keep its members aware of Co-operation without resort to some of the techniques of advertising, publicity and mass communication employed by competing interests. Moreover at this level the Movement has to aim at attracting the attention of prospective as well as present members.

Dr Otto Neurath, the Austrian sociologist, once remarked that it was impossible for anyone living in London to avoid being told by poster and newspaper advertisements that a certain beverage[1] 'is good for you'. If profit enterprise can achieve this result, how much more ought the Co-operative Movement to tell its members and the citizens at large, with no less inevitability, other things which are 'good' and probably better for them. Mass-communication media are expensive of course, but not so expensive in the long run as failure on the Movement's part to make its mission understood or to hold its ground in a competitive world. The question is really whether the Movement intends to survive or not. The Co-operative Presses of certain countries were on the right track when they decided many years ago to distribute their members' journals by post, as do some large primary societies their periodical reports, because they recognised that what the postman delivered was almost certainly read.

The importance of prompt, accurate and full information is enhanced by its intimate relation with democracy, which can hardly hope to operate in any Co-operative society unless matters of common concern are also matters of common knowledge among the members. The practice begun by the men of Rochdale of convening regular members' meetings to which the committee submitted reports on the society's operations and precise financial statements is still the general practice of all types of Co-operative. The evolution of the members' meeting has already been discussed in the chapter on Democracy, but from the standpoint of Education the important consideration is that through the very growth of membership, the members' meeting has declined as a medium of information and has had to be supplemented by the printed word which in its turn has been supplemented by other media including television and radio.

Noteworthy is the evolution of the Co-operative Press from periodic bulletins of the character of house organs towards, on the one hand, magazines serving less as media of specific Co-operative information than as windows for Co-operators on the world at large and, on the other, towards technical journals dealing with events and problems of management and administration of significance to special branches of the Movement or particular groups or classes of Co-operator. Inevitably, as both kinds of journal develop and add the discussion of policy to their news and information services, the more they help to broaden the outlook of Co-operators on the economic and social mixes within which their organisations live and move. Indeed, to every important type of Co-operative belongs its specific educational field which comprises enlightenment not only on the internal working of the Co-operative but also on its intended influence and effects on the external economy. Thus a consumers' Co-operative, in order to make its policy, strategy and tactics intelligible to its members, has to keep them continually aware of the consumers' place in the economy, the disabilities under which they labour when bargaining individually, whether under competitive or monopolistic conditions, as well as their actual and potential influence when they combine their purchasing power in Co-operatives.

A similar awareness, though from a different angle, needs to be developed in producers' Co-operatives whose members should understand the forces of demand and supply governing their markets in both the short and the long term, as well as the conditions on which their societies operate remuneratively in these markets. Similarly again, the members of a housing Co-operative should acquire through their society a general knowledge of the extent and character of the housing problems of their country and Co-operation's actual and possible role in their solution. The study of Co-operation in a vacuum has no kind of practical value or result. Co-operation only becomes significant against its economic and social background and without this knowledge Co-operators are prone to expect sometimes too much, sometimes too little, of their societies — for example, demanding dividends when conditions do not permit societies to earn them — and they may also fail to support their managements loyally in difficult situations or warn them effectively against possible mistakes.

Within the Co-operative Movement itself, if its educational work is well done, the consciousness of the typical Co-operator will not be bounded by the primary Co-operative of which he may be a member. From the very foundation of their Co-operative or from the moment of their entry into an old-established society, the members must be made aware that it is but a unit in a much larger movement. Office-bearers should be made acquainted as early as possible with neighbouring societies so that their minds are more or less prepared for collaboration and eventual federation before either becomes a practical necessity.

Sooner or later federation or amalgamation will appear on the agenda and the task of educationists is to anticipate and prepare for this. The alternative of federating first and attempting to educate after invites the virtually inevitable result that the outlook of the average member lags behind the actual situation. National problems will be encountered which the great body of Co-operators are able to grasp only from a local standpoint. That is in fact what has happened almost everywhere and it accounts to a great extent for the sluggishness with which Co-operative Movements have adopted the far-reaching measures of concentration and re-grouping made necessary by their transformed competitive situation. A similar but longer time-lag is to be observed on the international level and has much to do with the slow and irresolute development of inter-trading between Co-operative federations of different countries and Continents over the last 60 years. It is not that the Co-operative Movement's internationalism is not sincere, but that it remains for the most part on the plane of mere sentiment and is not informed and directed by real knowledge and understanding such as education alone can give.

Because Co-operation must be efficient in its own sense of the term, Co-operative Education necessarily includes an element of technical training. Many of the techniques employed in Co-operative business are little different, if at all, from those in use in any other form of undertaking engaged in the same branches of industry or commerce. Where training in these techniques is already provided by the State or the industry or by the two jointly, there is no reason for the Co-operative Movement to attempt to provide it independently. It has simply to insist that its employees and officials receive the training generally available. There is no substance in the assertion sometimes heard that this training must be given 'in a Co-operative atmosphere'. On the other hand, the Movement is obliged to train its personnel in those technical processes which are peculiar to Co-operative practice and which mostly result from the fact that a Co-operative consists of members and not mere shareholders. There are, for example, procedures for recording members' transactions with their societies and for the calculation and payment of sums due to them involved in the dividend system. Or again, the observance of the Principle of Democracy requires administrative and consultative 'machinery', the working of which must be understood, not only by a Co-operative's permanent officials, but also by its ordinary members and the officers they elect, if it is to fulfil its proper tasks and its rules are to be efficiently carried out.

The general assembly, for example, if it is to act effectively as the supreme authority in any Co-operative, must be familiar as to its purpose, powers, procedures and standing orders (where such exist) to a sufficiently large nucleus of members, otherwise it will tend to atrophy and with it, democracy in the society as a whole. In fact this machinery must become so familiar to all concerned that it can be handed over to what has been well called 'the effortless custody of habit'. But in order that habit shall not degenerate into routine, it is also necessary that members shall be competent to take full advantage of the opportunities for initiative which the general assembly may offer. When they have good ideas they should know how to put them forward and get them seriously discussed and ultimately voted upon. Technical skill and knowhow are indispensable. If they are not to be acquired by the slow and uncertain processes of trial and error, the society must provide training which must be within the reach of every member. The fact that only a minority will avail themselves of it is no argument against providing it. One of the great advantages of the guilds, youth groups and other voluntary associations encouraged within certain national Co-operative Movements is that they serve as training grounds in which the young and inexperienced can exercise themselves in debate, record-keeping, reporting, secretaryship and chairmanship and thereby acquire experience and confidence.

A man or woman, however, may be both knowledgeable about Co-operative affairs and, as member or official, a skilful manipulator of the Movement's economic and democratic machinery without being in the full sense an educated Co-operator, just as a performer on any instrument can be a proficient executant without being a thorough musician. Co-operative Education has therefore to be completed by the third element which we have called social discipline. This implies something more than the intellectual discipline represented by the social sciences which throw light upon Co-operative Principles and their application, although these disciplines are included in it. It includes also the study of Co-operation's underlying Principles and their mutual reconciliation, not in the abstract, but in the creation and development of Co-operative institutions offering solutions to fundamental economic and social problems of the contemporary world. Here is the common intellectual ground on which all Co-operators whatever their functions, whatever their background, must meet if the Movement is to achieve unity and hold together. The educated Co-operator must be capable of recognising the Co-operative idea in its endlessly diverse embodiments and of visualising the multitudes of Co-operative societies, unions, federations and other institutions as members of one family with a common allegiance.

The work of specialists, however well-trained and knowledgeable, and the discharge of particular functions, however necessary and efficient, are unproductive without a common centre of reference, a common inspiration in the same idea. Specialisation must be balanced and stabilised by co-ordination, otherwise it becomes a centrifugal destructive force. Just as Co-operatives in practice advance towards a unity growing ever more comprehensive, so must the study of Co-operation complement analysis by the synthesis of all those ideas which time and experience have confirmed to be of universal significance. As the social consciousness of the typical Co-operator expands from his local primary society to embrace the national and ultimately the international Co-operative Movement, so he begins to perceive, from the comparison of success and failure at different times in different places, what truths about Co-operation are of only local or only national significance and to distinguish between them and those others which are of universal application wherever genuine Co-operation exists.

But social discipline also includes the reverse face of the coin of which Co-operative Principles are the obverse, namely, standards of conduct for the individual. The members of the Movement, if they are collectively its masters, must be willing as individuals to serve it. They are in the last analysis the trustees of one another's welfare and a sense of trusteeship has not only to be developed by Education among Co-operative officers and officials, but also diffused as widely as possible among the general membership, along with the sentiment of brotherhood and mutual loyalty. There is another discipline to be learnt which may be called democratic and it consists in the honest and loyal operation of democratic procedures for consultation and decision and good-humoured acceptance of democratic decisions, when they have been fairly reached. It is not a defect in mankind to be ambitious for power or to believe fervently in the rightness of particular policies or doctrines. Yet it is inconsistent with good Co-operative standards of conduct to allow ambition to trample upon the rights of others or for fanaticism to suppress the beliefs and right to express them of others, or in the name of either opinion or doctrine to undermine democratic institutions or falsify democratic processes. Again, if freedom is to be maximised within Co-operative institutions, the attitude of individual members to one another must be one of tolerance and if Equity is to be achieved and maintained in changing circumstances, it can only be where Co-operators cultivate their sense of justice to the point where they recognise what is due to others as readily as they do what is due to themselves.

If the foregoing arguments are carried far enough, we cannot escape the conclusions that all Co-operators more or less and certainly all Co-operative educators must be something of philosophers and that Co-operative administrators, especially those likely to be called to occupy positions of authority in the national and international Co-operative Movements, must have the education of statesmen. Many in the past, with the requisite native ability, have made statesmen of themselves by learning from their varied experience. The Movement however, has often not reaped the full benefit of their wisdom because they arrived late in life in leading positions, and exercised their authority for only a few years before their retirement or death. One of the tasks of Co-operative educational systems, in whatever country or Continent, is to search for latent ability among Co-operators of all types and ages, and having found it to develop it and encourage its employment for the benefit of the Movement. Yet Education will be frustrated in its work if Co-operative administration is not far-sighted enough to take the ability disclosed in business operations, no less than by training courses and schools, and to keep open careers for talent. It is ultimately not in competition for trade, but in competition for ability, that the fate of the Co-operative Movement will be sealed.

CHAPTER NINE

Co-operative Principles and Social Progress

'Social progress' is a term requiring definition, otherwise it is liable to beg a multitude of questions. During the Co-operative Movement's period of development, people's ideas of progress have undergone a fundamental change. At the time when the basic types of Co-operative were being conceived and established in Europe, popular exponents of philosophy taught — and a great part of the public, including Co-operators, was ready to believe — that progress was inherent in the natural order and could not be set aside. The spread of evolutionary thought and the growth of wealth resulting from scientific discovery and technological invention induced a mood of optimism in which the notion of a law of progress found ready acceptance. 'Progress', wrote the English philosopher, Herbert Spencer, 'is not an accident but a necessity. What we call evil and immorality must disappear. It is certain that man must become perfect'.

Such breathtaking optimism seems today to be founded on much too narrow a basis of art, experience and history. It carries no conviction to a generation which has suffered two world wars, with their concomitant political and economic convulsions, and to another generation which lives now under the threat of nuclear annihilation. It is not surprising that many react to the opposite extreme, after the manner of the man who became a convinced pessimist through living too long among optimists, and deny the possibility of progress in the sense of any general or permanent improvement in the condition of mankind. Time has laid bare the crazy foundations of 19th century optimism. Progress results, not from any impersonal law of nature, but from human effort, according to the directions in which it is exerted.

Progress in certain directions may prevent or endanger progress in others. It is not merely that the progress in natural science, technology and industrial organisation, through which men in parts (but only parts) of the world have achieved a control over their physical environment hitherto unknown and scarcely conceivable, has been accomplished at the expense of needless human suffering and destruction of moral and cultural values. It has distracted and still distracts attention and interest from the solution of the human and social problems inevitably engendered by technical and industrial revolutions. Mankind is prone to take the line of least resistance: it seems easier to control natural forces than human desires, easier to calculate quantities than to distinguish between qualities, easier to send astronauts into orbit than to make scores of millions of men, women and children secure from hunger.

Herbert Spencer's affirmation of the perfectibility of mankind seems as unfounded as his belief in a law of progress. The improvement of society, likewise the improvement of the individual, can result only from determined effort and the choice of the appropriate methods of education and organisation and, even then, its possibilities are subject to severe limitations of time and place. In any event, what is improvement? By what standards are we to judge better or worse? Towards what goals do we wish to advance? Despite the development of the social sciences, there is probably no entirely objective answer to be given to those questions. Value judgements are unavoidable, but this is not necessarily a fatal disadvantage if we are aware of what they are and from what standpoint they are made.

The line of progress which has brought Western society, and the rest of mankind along with it, to the brink of destruction by nuclear war is not one that any reflective man or woman would wish to pursue. Why then do the nations still linger on the brink? One answer may be that war, preparations for war and mutual deterrence against attack are endemic in an economic and social system in which the capitalistic motive, gain through investment, is the main driving force. These must also represent a serious risk in a world distracted by the competitive co-existence of opposed ideological and power systems. If that is not the complete answer, but only a part of it, another part may be that mankind and its leaders persist in applying to the issues of the 20th century the intellectual instruments and ideas of the 19th and yet earlier centuries.

Anyone can see with hindsight how the pre-Industrial Revolution economics of Adam Smith were applied with disastrous social results to post-Industrial Revolution problems, but our generation is committing a similar blunder by attempting to force problems demanding co-operation on a world scale into the straitjacket of ideas of national sovereignty and aggrandisement, regardless of the fact that these have already plunged the world into two calamitous wars within 30 years. What is worse, the newly-liberated peoples seem intent on copying the behaviour of the senior nation-States whose example is, of course, always more convincing than their precept.

But how should the newly-developing States learn when the old-established governments, while preaching co-operation, practise competition and 'sacred egoism' and while contributing money to international organisations, frustrate their work by preferring national to international solutions? The tension between the fact of increasing interdependence and the cult of nationalism again and again inhibits international action, whether to maintain peace, restore order, restrain warlike preparations, stimulate the flow of trade or stabilise the currency exchanges. Statesmen with a world vision can achieve a modicum of international collaboration only by trimming their policies to the self-interest of their unenlightened constituents or by making concessions to the cupidity of pressure-groups. Schizophrenia would seem to be the most common ailment in what George Bernard Shaw once called 'the planetary lunatic asylum'.

There is in fact only one way in which the world can retire from the danger zone of nuclear destruction and that is the path, indicated by the old Owenites, of 'unrestrained Co-operation for every purpose of social life'. Neither the individual nor the social order can be improved, apart from Co-operative effort. Social progress depends upon and consists in continually increasing men's capacity for Co-operation and the effectiveness of their performance in Co-operative action. An amiable cynic once remarked that the chief differences between man and the other animals were his use of cooked food and of articulate speech. The present writer would add a third difference even more important than the other two, and that is man's greater capacity for organised collaboration. The true line of progress lies in the enlargement of these differences, and especially the third. But if men are to work together whole-heartedly and successfully on whatever scale, they must be able to agree on common objects, the selection of their organisers and leaders, the method of sharing the benefits, as well as be willing to train themselves in the appropriate techniques — all this to achieve co-operation (with the small 'c'). If they are to succeed at co-operation they can hardly leave out of account the Principles of Co-operation (with the capital 'C'). Here we may perhaps catch a glimpse of the relation between the economic and social macrocosm and the microcosm of the Co-operative Movement, as well as what the French Socialist leader Jean Jaures meant by his famous comparison of the Movement to a laboratory for the study of the problems of future society. Co-operation between nations must rest on a foundation of Co-operation within nations.

To link co-operation with Co-operation in this way is not to forget, contradict or diminish the differences between them pointed out at the very beginning of this study. On the contrary, it is to emphasise that, if co-operation is to achieve even greater effectiveness and success, especially on the international level, it will be obliged more and more to imitate and resemble that synthesis of Association with other universal Principles represented by the techniques and doctrines of Co-operation. In the social climate of today, people attempting to work together sooner or later risk self-frustration unless they can persuade not only their collaborators but society at large that their collaboration results in economy rather than waste, is democratic rather than dictatorial in its organisation and spirit, checks exploitation and reinforces social justice, promotes social responsibility in the exercise of power, and extends rather than diminishes personal freedom. Nevertheless much co-operation is still improvised, sporadic, amateurish in method and restricted in outlook. It could become much more systematic and stable, besides immeasurably more competent, if it could borrow from the arsenal of methods, techniques and structures which the Co-operative Movement has accumulated in its long practical experience of social organisation.

Before passing on to consider what specific contributions Co-operative Principles may offer to social progress, we may recall how contemporary society is behaving in the fundamental and universal situations briefly mentioned in the discussion of the Principles in Chapter One. It is one of the commonplaces of our time that the evolution of science, technology and the arts of administration and management is leading the world more and more into situations where Association in some form or other is inevitable in this sense: that it appears to be the only course which people of intelligence and goodwill could contemplate. Advantages beckon in the shape of savings and gains effected through large-scale operation. New administrative techniques and equipment such as computers facilitate concentration. The necessity of ensuring and maintaining the yield of massive capital investments acts as a driving force. All combine to bring about interdependence and encourage integration in ever larger units, be they co-ordinated transport or power systems on the national level or, on the international, the customs unions, free trade areas and common markets in which national markets may come to be merged, to say nothing of the old-established groups and concerns such as operate in the petroleum, edible oil, chemical, automobile and electrical industries and exert a powerful influence in all the world's important markets. Competition is not eliminated, but its scope and force are considerably modified by the growing preference for association, agreement and organised control in more or less permanent forms.

This tendency has been reinforced by the extension of government activity in economic affairs, not so much in the form of State-created or State-sponsored enterprise as in the form of consultation, initiative, regulation and forward planning. In these conditions, emphasis tends to shift from considerations of simple profitability to the prosperity of the whole national economy and the prospective role, increasing or declining, of any given industry in it. There thus develops on the part of both government and industry, a fuller recognition of the functional principle and among leaders of industry, commerce and banking, as well as their various chambers and federations, a keener sense of their responsibilities from the social point of view.

With that comes a broader conception of the proper aim of industrial and commercial enterprise as being not merely profits but the widest possible diffusion of economic well-being. Here emerge those considerations of social justice which the Co-operative Pioneers called Equity. Granted that the size of private incomes within a national economy must bear some relation to the growth and productivity of that economy, there still remain the problems of distributing income between those who contribute capital and those contributing labour or professional skill, between those working for home and those working for export markets, between industry and agriculture and so forth. In Great Britain, for example, the implementation of a national incomes policy, if it were to imply restraint on demands for higher wages and salaries, could only be workable if it entailed control of interest and profit rates also.

The concentration of power and the growth of responsibility at the summit of the economic system are not necessarily accompanied by an increase, and may be accompanied by a decline, of responsibility at the base. In fact, as the seat of power becomes more remote, loss of participation in control may lead to repudiation of responsibility. There is a discordance, still to be resolved, between democracy in politics and hierarchy in industry. The term plutodemocracy is not unjustified when it is applied to societies which give people as citizens rights of consultation, besides imposing duties of decision, on matters of which they have little or no direct knowledge, and at the same time refuse them to people as workers on matters within their daily and year-long working experience. This antimony creates tensions which check or hinder production through stoppages and in numerous other ways. The dilemma is critical; if the co-operation of the workers is needed by management (and it surely is), then democracy cannot be in the long run excluded from industrial organisation — or if it is, then democracy in politics will fade away into demagogy, ultimately tempered by dictatorship.

The price of democracy, as of liberty, is eternal vigilance. Any kind of democracy decays unless it is constantly renewed and re-animated by education, just as any economic system will lapse into inefficiency for the same reason. Social progress, therefore, is unthinkable and unattainable apart from cultivation of the abilities and characters of individual men and women, the enrichment of their knowledge of their physical and social environment, the development of their manual and intellectual skills, the sharpening of their perceptions and judgements, the broadening of their sympathies, and their training in self and social responsibility.

Yet the contribution which education is now making to true democracy and social progress in general is much smaller than it might be and than it must, as soon as possible, become. Education is betrayed by its internal weaknesses, as well as handicapped by external obstacles. Much of it is still backward — rather than forward — looking in both content and method; it has not yet absorbed, still less applied, what the psychologists have revealed about the importance of the years children spend before they go to school; it is still prone to premature and improperly balanced specialisation in the studies of adolescents; it is oriented more towards individual acquisitiveness and careerism than towards social service. Externally, education of any kind has to struggle continually against hostile influences which are often in the short run more powerful. The conflict may be typified by the schoolchild's hesitation (or lack of it) between homework and television, the latter standing for the whole genus of commercialised pleasures and distractions which, if not in fact deleterious, are no more than mere pastimes, contributing nothing to the growth of the mind and personality.

For this purpose commercialism has too often appropriated education's proper tools. A kindred type of mis-education is the abuse of mass-communication media for either profit-making or political ends. The object is to sway people in masses, either to build up the markets required for profitable mass-production or to condition them into conformity with a given policy or ideology. Herdmindedness is accordingly strengthened at the expense of the individual judgement and conscience. Shrinking from social inferiority or ostracism, people keep up with their neighbours or go along with the crowd. The noble conception of the sovereign people declines into mob-rule. The truth of any superstition is regarded as proved by the millions of people who can be persuaded to believe it. The deliberate use of mob-demonstrations by anti-democratic governments in certain countries and by anti-democratic parties elsewhere is significant in this connection. The choice before the world, as Ch. H. Barbier[1] rightly declared to the ICA Press and Education Conference in 1963, is between a mass and a Cooperative civilisation. This is not a choice which concerns only the nations of advanced economic development. Third World nations have the same difficult decision to make as to the direction of their social, economic and political evolution.

The circumstances, of course, differ considerably in the two cases. If an over-simplified distinction may be drawn, for the sake of brevity, between the 'affluent' and the 'indigent' societies, the chief difference may perhaps be stated as follows: the affluent societies are still carried along in a direction determined by the momentum of their previous technical and industrial development, competitively increasing their volume and means of production, although they have reached the point where the output of necessities greatly exceeds need, and quality, rather than quantities, should be the aim; whereas the indigent are still in the stage where their greatest immediate need is the most rapid expansion possible of their output, either of primary necessities or of commodities easily exchangeable in foreign markets for such necessities.

The affluent, despite many years of effort, either directly or through international organisations, to provide technical aid and capital, have failed to narrow the gap between their own standards of comfort and those of the indigent societies. The well-fed nations are still greater food-producers than the under-fed. Those with wealth accumulate still more, those without tend to sink deeper in poverty and, where freedom of movement is still possible, export their wholly or partly unemployed labour to countries of over-full employment. No one dares to deny the celebrated dictum of the International Labour Organisation that 'poverty anywhere is a menace to prosperity everywhere,' but attempts to free the exchanges and build an equitable system of distribution so as to give the indigent more favourable terms of trade are frustrated again and again by the vested interests in production of the affluent and their unwillingness to sacrifice their actual or prospective gains under the present system. Not until and unless a more abundant life, conceived as the liberation of the human spirit for the pursuit of loftier ends, rather than the accumulation of the means to and appurtenances of living, becomes the general goal and object of emulation, will the affluent nations be able to free themselves from enslavement to their possessions and what American poet Walt Whitman called 'the mania of owning things'.

Their problem is to gain control of the processes which have carried them to the giddy verge of catastrophe and divert them so that they minister to mankind's spiritual fulfilment. It may be remarked in passing that there seems no great difference — and that only a difference of degree — between the nations with mixed and the nations with centrally-planned economies. What is significant is the ever-greater concern for consumers' interests and satisfactions manifested in both types of economy and the evidence it gives that both are following much the same course towards the same end: an overwhelmingly material and materialistic superabundance, a plethora of things measurable by statistics.

The indigent nations, on the other hand, require, as the first step in their progress, a great increase of material wealth, especially in forms ministering more or less directly to the preservation of physical life — food, shelter, medical care and so on. Their peoples must be adequately nourished, protected from the elements by good housing, trained in hygiene, relieved from drudgery, so that their working capacity and their expectation of life may greatly increase. But even in their present stage of development they cannot evade the question of means and ends. Granted that they would be free from hunger and insecurity, exploitation and alien oppression, what would they be free to do and to become? They cannot postpone their search for their answers to this question, for men's characters are formed, not only by what they do, but also by how they do it. Already the old cultures are crumbling. Ancient social custom and tribal authority are yielding place to modern systems of government and administration. The desertion of the countryside continues irresistibly as the need for higher incomes impels the menfolk, accompanied or followed by their families, to seek a living among the rootless proletariat of the growing seaports, mining camps and centres of transport and manufacture, where their very poverty will prevent them from absorbing anything but the dregs of Western cultures, commercially supplied.

The foremost thinkers of the developing nations, who have contact with the wider world, have insight enough to realise that there is little virtue in mere imitation, that political liberty loses its value unless it sets them free to develop according to their national or racial genius. The African and the Asian must maintain their own originality, not barter it in order to become copies of the European or American. Some of their politicians on the morrow of liberation from colonial rule pointed to the democratic Welfare State as the proper goal of a united national effort. But more than a few political leaders have found that the national unity, built up in order to throw off alien rule, has had to be created anew under conditions of self-government. It is much easier to acquire the trappings of nationality than to develop a sense of nationhood among disparate tribal and racial elements. In any event, nations grow in cohesion only as their citizens come to recognise their common interests and acquire the knack and the habit of working together. Unless the indigent societies are willing and able to cooperate they will not attain the Welfare States of their dreams or accomplish anything else of truly human value. Their material progress may be slow at first, but that very fact offers the opportunity of controlling it and subordinating it to human needs, before it grows strong enough to impose its own limited and lop-sided values on society.

Broadly speaking, there are two ways in which Co-operative Principles can influence social progress. One is obviously through the spread of Co-operative institutions and the enlargement of their scope and economic power. The other is through the projection of Co-operative ideas upon the wider economic and social world and its evolution. Within the last 20 years, the Co-operative Movement has attained world-wide extension. Its further progress should consist more and more in the intensive development of Co-operative sectors within national economies through the growth of existing Co-operative organisations; the application of Co-operative methods to diverse fields of economic activity and to new problems as they arise; the consolidation and integration of the various types of Co-operative; and closer economic and moral links between the Co-operative Movements of different countries and Continents under the fostering care of the International Co-operative Alliance. No limits can be set *a priori* to this development which is bound to be affected and in some ways determined by what happens simultaneously in the private (capitalist) and public sectors with which the Co-operative is, in a certain measure in competition, although complementary to them.

At this point in the argument it seems necessary and appropriate to refer to the present position and state of the world-wide Co-operative Movement, the most important part of which is enrolled in the International Co-operative Alliance. The aggregate individual membership of the Alliance is now some 500 million in about 70 countries. The most striking fact about this membership is its diversity. It is not simply that Co-operatives have been formed by all sorts of people for almost all sorts of purposes, but that they differ in size and age and social and economic background. Some societies are well over 100 years old, others less than a dozen. Some national organisations number their members in scores of millions, others in a few thousand. The one common element is adherence to the Co-operative idea, but whether that means the same to all of them it may be permissible to doubt. One object of analysing the Co-operative idea into its component Principles is to help towards a common understanding between all Co-operatives, those already existing and those to come.

The influence of the Co-operative Movement on social progress depends very largely, and will depend even more in the future, on its unity at different levels, especially the national and international. It will also depend on the power of Co-operative Movements to make headway against competition, to adapt themselves to economic and social changes which they can neither withstand nor control and, in short, to survive in an environment different from that in which they were formed. In Europe, where the Movement began, there are already signs of a loss of dynamism in a disinclination to make changes and a tendency to persist in old ways when they obviously will not meet the needs of the present. When that happens, Co-operation loses its superiority and with it its power to hold its members and attract new ones. This will be seen in its loss of market share or membership or both.

In Great Britain and in Germany, consumer Co-operatives were experimenting with self-service as early as 1950, but apparently without realising that it was not simply a new method of handling goods and cash, but the spearhead of a revolution which was going to transform retail trading. Swedish Co-operators were probably the first who appreciated what would happen. Sweden was neutral during the war and the Swedes had been able to keep in touch with what was happening in America. It was they who moved the resolution at the Copenhagen ICA Congress that set up a Rationalisation Committee. They also kept watch on the Swiss entrepreneur Gottlieb Duttweiler, who not merely converted his system of travelling vans into self-service stores but sought to bind his customers by offering them shares and consulting them on policy, converting his company into a Co-operative in Swiss law. Duttweiler was far from being the only trader who could forecast the future. Private shopkeepers all over Europe banded themselves together in 'voluntary chains' and within a year or two formed an international association.

With the consumers' Co-operative Movement, however, consolidation was — and is — a process strung out over decades and in some countries is not yet completed. There was not merely reluctance to amalgamate, there was resistance, almost to the point of liquidation. In Holland that point was passed and two-thirds of the consumers' Co-operatives were privatised in one way or another. In Denmark, a scheme of amalgamation was not completed before the wholesale federation FDB had to appeal for help to its Scandinavian neighbours. In Western Germany, the consumers' Co-operatives were saved by the intervention of the trade union bank and the adoption of the company form of enterprise (with a few notable exceptions of which Dortmund is the chief). The bank controlled most of the rest as a group through a holding company called the Coop Zentrale Aktiengesellschaft.

By contrast, in two of Europe's smaller countries, the consumers' Co-operative Movement has apparently successfully carried the process of consolidation through to the national stage. They are Switzerland and Austria, and their national organisations are known respectively as Coop Schweiz or Coop Suisse and Coop Austria. It is no mere coincidence that these two Movements are remarkable for the high standard of their educational work, more especially in management training. Not that the membership is neglected. The Austrian system of member participation has already been mentioned in an earlier chapter. The Swiss Movement is noteworthy for its members' journals which are published weekly in newspaper form, with a total circulation that compares very favourably with the aggregate individual membership.

Turning to Great Britain one cannot but deplore the apparent inability of the Movement to make up its mind what it wishes to become. Some Co-operators believe that a national consumers' Co-operative society is both desirable and inevitable. Others believe in a regional system and the figure of regional societies has been officially mentioned, although it is not entirely clear whether the figure is but notional. Others again seem incapable of thinking about a change of structure until affairs reach a stage when the choice is either liquidation or a transfer of engagements. There is also the unique phenomenon of Co-operative Retail Services which is neither national nor regional but a last refuge for non-viable societies in any part of the country, its membership growing as the number of societies diminishes. What seems certain is that the British Movement let the best time for change and restructuring slip by when the economy was still booming and societies were financially stronger than they now are after years of depression. How the Movement will come through and in what shape is not possible for me to predict.

The general impression is that in the European market economies the consumers' Co-operatives find it hard to hold their ground or make headway against the aggression of the retail competition. They would do well to confer more than they do at present. In fact, they might do worse than set up a common institute whose function would be to regain and retain for the whole Movement its superiority in retail trade. The Scandinavian countries would have much to contribute to a pool of information and ideas, and the countries like Greece, Spain and Portugal, where consumers' Co-operation is still in its early stages, could draw information and inspiration from it. What is needed is an institute whose researches would cover all economic and social movements which are likely to affect the forms and methods of retail trade, whose experts would give technical advice of every kind which would help to raise the standards of Co-operative retailing, while giving practical help and encouragement to those organisations which encountered special difficulties. The object in view all the time is to trade successfully, while sticking to the Principles of Co-operation.

There is probably no better example of success in Europe than the Society with its headquarters at Dortmund in West Germany. In 1982 this Society increased its turnover by 10.2 per cent, with an increase in market share, and added 20,000 new members to make a total of 355,000. It paid a dividend on purchases of between 2 per cent and 3 per cent, in addition to interest of 11 per cent on share capital. In the course of

1983 it added 823 persons (495 being apprentices) to its staff of 8,151. To quote the eminent German Co-operator Dr Erwin Hasselmann: 'Co-op Dortmund is the living proof that a Co-operative controlled by consumers and well managed can not merely maintain its position but also come victorious out of the battle with the most powerful and aggressive of competitors.' If consumers' Co-operatives throughout Europe were working at the Dortmund standard there would be little cause for anxiety.

It is remarkable how the very depression has brought about a revival of interest in forms of Co-operation other than consumers', more especially in the countries of the European Economic Community in which unemployment is rife and prospects of re-employment are bleak. In Great Britain, workers' Co-operatives have proliferated with the help of the Government's Co-operative Development Agency and the assistance and advice of other Co-operative bodies. Housing Co-operatives have greatly increased in numbers following the example set by most European countries and the United States. Credit Unions, introduced mainly by West Indian and Irish immigrants, are gaining ground. Co-operation has become fashionable for a number of other purposes, and steps are being taken, with the support of the Co-operative Development Agency, to bring the various types of Co-operatives into closer and mutually helpful relations.

In France, Belgium and even West Germany, redundant workers without other hope are seeking to employ themselves by mutual aid. In France especially, the Government attaches considerable value to workers' Co-operative production as a means of counteracting local unemployment. But there exist also two things which could be copied with advantage by other countries. The first is an organisation called the Groupement National de la Coopération which embraces every known type of Co-operative and enables them to communicate on all matters of common interest and, where necessary and practicable, to take action in common. The second is the recognition by the Socialist Government of the Co-operative Movement as the most important element of what is called 'the social economy', which is different in nature from both the private and public sectors of the economy and therefore requires different legislative and administrative treatment.

However, Co-operative Movements in our time need not only to unite on the national level and receive appropriate recognition from national states, they need also to be able to influence supra-national authorities of which the European Economic Community is one example. The national consumers' Co-operative federations in the EEC have been associated in Euro-Coop for over 20 years and the Agricultural Co-operatives in COGECA. Other types of Co-operative have followed their example. They are now agreed in principle that for some purposes they should all act together, otherwise Co-operation may well be ignored by the EEC or find itself subject to some form of EEC company legislation.

At the world level, the Co-operative Movement is represented at the United Nations by the International Co-operative Alliance which has consultative status with the Economic and Social Council. Its huge aggregate membership gives it broader popular support than any other consultative body. Consultative status means much more than the right to attend Council meetings, suggest questions for the agenda and submit oral and written statements. It includes among many other privileges the right to attend meetings of the Regional Economic Councils which serve the different Continents, and the meetings of special Committees of the Council, as well as to receive all kinds of information on matters coming before the Council. The ICA has similar consultative status with the International Labour Office, the Food and Agriculture Organisation and UNESCO, the United Nations Educational, Scientific and Cultural Organisation. The ICA thus has numberless opportunities of exerting influence on behalf of the Movement and many different ways of furthering the cause of Co-operation — more opportunities in fact than it has the power and resources to exploit. It has never been adequately funded by its members' subscriptions for the tasks it is expected to perform and has had to rely too much on help from friendly governments, the ILO, the UN and certain affiliated national

Co-operative organisations to finance many of its projects.

The removal of the headquarters of the Alliance to Geneva and the consequent close proximity to the Co-operative Department of the International Labour Office open up possibilities of closer collaboration which should be of great benefit to both of them, besides offering opportunities of tackling some problems on a global scale. One of the most deplorable features of the present world-wide economic depression is the failure of both public and private enterprise to find any common bases from which to start a return to prosperity or even to alleviate the depression's worst effects. The number of undernourished, to say nothing of starving, people in the world does not diminish. Of the millions unemployed there is a high proportion who can never expect to work for wages again among the old, and there is an equally high proportion among the young who have had to leave school without the slightest prospect of employment. The very helplessness of governments and entrepreneurs is a reason why Co-operators, like their ancestors who pioneered Co-operative Movements in the last century, should bestir themselves in whatever kind of Co-operative action which offers hope of relief.

Dr Alexander Laidlaw[2] in his well-known report *Co-operatives in the Year 2,000* suggested four areas in which Co-operatives should find scope for action and development — feeding a hungry world, workers' Co-operative production, conservation, and urban community planning. The first conjures up a vision of a great coalition of the ICA, the FAO and the IFAP with the great agricultural supply and marketing federations and the consumers' wholesale societies, taking a section of the world at a time and working out on their several levels a system extending from cultivation and stock-rearing to marketing and processing, storage and distribution, which would allow where necessary for import and export, all running on Co-operative lines and aiming at being eventually self-financing.

We have seen in the last 20 years a new start in workers' Co-operative production, which is still largely struggling to find its feet, but should be encouraged to think of long-term development and self-finance. But they should also federate for all matters in which they have a common interest and ally themselves with other types of Co-operative, forging international links. Societies for conservation and other community Societies are increasing in numbers and should be supported as a counterpoise to local and national bureaucracy.

Of course for any of these aims to be realised the Co-operative Movement has to fulfil certain conditions. Co-operators must be clear in their minds about their Principles and the reasons why they must preserve them intact, not like stuffed animals in a natural history museum, but alive through continual renewal in the birth of new Co-operative entities and structures which meet the demands of changing times. Again, as nearly as human frailty and fallibility allow, the Movement's practice must illustrate and faithfully exemplify its Principles. Co-operators must pursue efficiency in every branch of the Movement's activity with no less persistence and ruthlessness than their opponents who work for profits. They may conceive efficiency in different terms from those of the capitalist and entrepreneur but they have to prove the validity of their Principles in action, by showing that Co-operation works, delivers the goods and manifestly honours the claims they make for it.

Where confusion prevails about the Principles, especially where they are controlled and appear to be falsified by practice, Co-operation has no safeguard against degeneration or perversion. The common bond that unites Co-operators everywhere and serves as the basis of their international collaboration would dissolve. The Movement would lose its only assurance that it can preserve its identity in a world of change and face the certainty that the more it changes, the less (not the more) it will remain the same thing. Inevitably the Co-operative sector will tend to imitate and reproduce the private and public sectors and when it can do no more than that, it will be due to be absorbed by them or swept into the dustbin of history. Co-operation can find no neutral state between advance and retreat, expansion or decline.

There seems no justification, when the growth of the Co-operative Movement is surveyed in retrospect against the background of the world's economic, social and political history during the last 200 years, for thinking that it has passed its zenith and is due to wane before its greatest mission has been discharged. Despite world wars and economic depressions, the collapse of empires and the re-drawing of national boundaries, political repression and persecution, the Co-operative idea, with all its setbacks, has survived to become more relevant than ever and has continually increased the number of its adherents in most parts of the habitable globe. Even in the countries where the position of the Co-operative Movement is most furiously assailed by large-scale capitalist competition which may appear to have halted its advance, it still possesses material, intellectual and moral reserves which have not yet been fully mobilised, to say nothing of deployed. In the regions where it is the only agency capable of leading the people step by step out of a natural into an exchange economy, training them to play an active and responsible part in their own social progress and enabling them to make with success the transition from tribal to national and international solidarity, it has work before it for generations to come.

Notes

Preface

1. Edward Vansittart Neale (1810–1892) Christian Socialist; promoter of workers' Co-operative productive societies; first General Secretary of the British Co-operative Union from 1873 to 1890; joint author of *A Manual for Co-operators*, a classic of Co-operative ethics and economics.
2. Henry J. May (1866–1939) Parliamentary Secretary of the Co-operative Union from 1908 to 1922; General Secretary of the International Co-operative Alliance from the Glasgow ICA Congress (1913) until his death.

Chapter One

1. Horace Plunkett (1854–1932) pioneer of agricultural Co-operation in Ireland who after 40 meetings established the first Irish Co-operative creamery. His lifework is commemorated by the Plunkett Foundation for Co-operative Studies, Oxford.
2. G.J. Holyoake (1817–1906) Co-operative leader and secularist. A prolific author of books on Co-operation. His opinions as a Freethinker and atheist led to his imprisonment in 1842. A founder of the British Co-operative Union, his name has been given to the Union's headquarters in Manchester.
3. Georges Fauquet (1883–1953) Doctor of medicine. First chief of the Co-operative Section of the International Labour Office; author of *The Co-operative Sector*.
4. Robert Owen (1771–1858) often described as 'The Father of Co-operation', his Co-operative ideas provided a stimulus to the Rochdale Pioneers and many other Co-operators. A prolific author on Co-operative and related questions. Founded a number of Co-operative communities but without success. Active also as an educationist, advocate of factory legislation and a founder of British trade unionism.

5. F. C. M. Fourier (1772–1837) French socialist who advocated the establishment of self-supporting Co-operative communities called 'phalanxes', the members living in a beautiful and commodious centre called a 'phalanstery'. Many Fourierist communities were started in France and the USA but did not succeed.
6. Charles Gide (1847–1932) Professor of Political Economy in several French universities and Professor of Co-operation in Paris in the 1920's. In his economic writings he emphasised the importance of the consumer.

Chapter Two

1. William Thompson (1785?–1833) Owenite Socialist and author of books defending the workers' right to the whole produce of their labour and giving practical directions for the formation of Co-operative communities.
2. Dr William King (1786–1865) Brighton physician and Co-operative thinker who wrote and published the famous *The Co-operator*, a monthly tract which appeared from May 1825 to August 1830. This four-page publication had great influence on early Co-operators and was certainly read by some of the Rochdale Pioneers.
3. Claude Henri Saint-Simon (1760–1825) French philosopher who taught that individualism and social strife must be superseded by association and social organisation.
4. Philippe Buchez (1794–1863) originally a disciple of Saint-Simon but became an advocate of working men's productive associations for those whose industries had not yet been mechanised.
5. Hermann Schulze-Delitzsch (1808–1883) from 1849 onwards organised German artisans in Co-operative credit societies known as 'people's banks' and purchasing associations for raw materials. He was a great popular educator and his Co-operative Movement spread rapidly in Germany and Austria where it is still strong today.
6. Friedrich Wilhelm Raiffeisen (1818–1888) provincial administrator who organised credit relief for poverty-stricken and indebted German peasantry. Between 1849 and 1862 he worked out a suitable form of credit society based on Co-operative self-help. This grew into the largest Co-operative Movement in Germany. Since 1920 Co-operative credit societies have been established in many other parts of the world.
7. J.C. Gray (1854–1912) appointed General Secretary of the British Co-operative Union in 1891. Was joint honorary secretary of the ICA. Advocated that all existing British Co-operative societies be combined into one national society.
8. E. Poisson (1882–1942) eminent French Co-operative leader and author. Became Secretary of the French Co-operative Union in 1912 and was eventually appointed Vice-President of the ICA — an office he

held until his death. His *Co-operative Republic* was translated into English by W.P. Watkins.

Chapter Three

1. Samuel Johnson (1709–1784) author, essayist, poet and critic. Compiler of the great *Dictionary of the English Language*. Subject of James Boswell's *Life of Samuel Johnson*, regarded as the greatest biography in English literature.
2. Dr J.B. Tayler, Christian missionary and lecturer in mathematics at Chinese universities. Took an active interest in the Co-operative marketing of cotton in China.
3. Albert Thomas (1879–1932) French Socialist politician and Co-operator. Director of the International Labour Office 1920–1932. Created the Co-operative Section of the ILO and appointed Dr Fauquet to head it.
4. John Maynard Keynes (1883–1946) British economist. Originator of the economic theory of 'Keynesianism' which had great influence on monetary and employment policy in Britain and elsewhere after the Second World War.

Chapter Four

1. Marcel Brot (1887–1966) eminent French Co-operator. He was simultaneously President of the Co-operators of Lorraine, President of the National Federation of Consumers' Co-operatives of France and from 1955 to 1960 President of the International Co-operative Alliance.
2. Independent Commission of Inquiry. Set up by the British Co-operative Movement in 1955, it was headed by Hugh Gaitskell, then leader of the Labour Party, with C.A.R. Crosland, later Foreign Minister, as Secretary. The Commission reported in 1959 on the Movement's main weaknesses and put forward radical proposals for its reorganisation.
3. Laiteries Réunies. United Dairies — the milk producer in partnership with the Geneva consumers' Co-operative.

Chapter Five

1. Nassau Senior (1790–1864) British economist whose theoretical writings are still held in esteem but whose practical proposals earned him the justified criticism of Karl Marx and others.

Chapter Eight

1. This beverage is an Irish black beer produced under the trade name of Guinness. The advertising slogan 'Guinness is good for you' became famous throughout Britain and Ireland, although it would not be allowed under current advertising legislation.

Chapter Nine

1. Charles Henri Barbier (1901–1984) French by birth but resident in Switzerland. Vice-President of the Swiss Co-operative Union and member of the ICA Executive Committee which he represented on UNESCO.
2. Dr Alex Laidlaw (1908–1980) General Secretary of the Co-operative Union of Canada. Served on the Central and Executive Committees of the ICA and was appointed to prepare a keynote paper on 'Co-operatives in the Year 2000'. His forecasts and warnings made a profound impression on the subsequent ICA Congress in Moscow (1980).

General

Since the text of this book was written, structural changes in the French Movement have meant that the federal organisation Fédération Nationale des Coopératives de Consommateurs has ceased to exist.

Index

Accounting, 47, 49, 103-104, 105
Advertising, 59, 100, 125
Aesop, 112
Africa —
   Co-operative Marketing, 47
Agricultural Co-operation, 12-13, 21, 22, 23, 27, 29, 30, 32-33, 37, 38, 40, 41, 47, 49, 50, 51, 64, 65, 71, 78, 88-90, 95, 99, 101, 129, 154, 155
Alexander, Gemmell, ix
Amalgamation, 57, 103, 106, 134, 151
America —
   Consumers Co-operative Association, 19, 26, 28
   Co-operative League of the USA, 19
   Credit Unions, 42
   Housing Co-operatives, 40; 153
   Insurance, 70-71
   Mutual Service Co-operative, 70-71
Aristotle, 73
Ashworth, Samuel, 81
Association or Unity, 10, 13, 15, 16, 18-35, 52, 72, 92, 97, 101, 102, 115, 142, 143
Audit Unions, 49, 103-104
Australia —
   Co-operative Marketing, 95
Austria —
   Co-operation, 60-61, 106, 151
   Co-operative Legislation, 103

Banking —
   Artisans People's Banks, 22
   Co-operative Bank, 43
   Credit Unions, 21, 22, 27, 42, 43, 55, 78, 90, 119-120, 153

   West German Trade Union Bank, 151
Barbier, Ch. H., 146
Bargaining Power, 22, 24, 25-26, 38, 39, 44, 50, 76, 99, 115
Belgium —
   Co-operation, 98, 153
Bonus to Employees, 82, 83, 86
Book-Keeping, 47, 49, 103-104, 105
Braun, Theo, 119-121
Brot, Marcel, 58-59, 63
Buchez, Philippe, 21

Canada —
   Co-operative Education, 127
   Direct Charge System, 45
   Wheat Pools, 27, 50, 89, 95
Capital, Limited Interest on, 6, 8, 76, 77-78, 79-91, 96
Carlyle, Thomas, 111
Cash Payments in Buying and Selling, 2, 6, 9, 41-43, 105
Central Co-operative Agency, Britain, 25
Centrosoyus, USSR, 4
China —
   Agricultural Co-operation, 41
Christian Socialists, 81
Clarke, Peter, ix
Clayton, Wilson, xii
Cleuet, A.J., viii
Colombain, Maurice, ix
Communism --
   Co-operation in Communist Countries, 3-4, 78
Congress --
   British, 70, 103

International Co-operative Alliance, 4-5, 7, 9-10, 19, 150
International Co-operative Congress 1895, 27
National, 70, 102
Consumer Credit, 2, 6, 9, 41-43, 76, 119-120
Consumers Co-operative Association, USA, 19, 26, 28
Co-operation Between Co-operatives, 19, 25, 30-35, 102
Co-operative Bank, Britain, 43
Co-operative Co-partnership Societies, 82
Co-operative Development Agency, Britain, 153
Co-operative Independent Commission, Britain, 62, 103
Co-operative League of the USA, 19

Co-operative Principles —
Association or Unity, 10, 13, 15, 16, 18-35, 52, 72, 92, 97, 101, 102, 115, 142, 143
Authority, 10, 13-17
Capital, Limited Interest on, 6, 8, 76, 77-78, 79-91, 96
Cash Payments in Buying and Selling, 2, 6, 9, 41-43, 105
Definition, 2
Democratic Control, 2, 6, 8, 9, 11, 13, 16, 17, 19, 54-72, 93, 105, 106-107, 120, 121, 131, 132, 135, 137, 142-143, 144-146
Dividend, 6, 8, 10-11, 44-45, 52, 73-74, 76-91, 105, 134, 135
Economy, 10, 13, 17, 36-53
Education, 2, 6, 8, 9, 11, 13, 17, 88, 123-138, 145-146, 151
Equity, 13, 15, 17, 73-91, 95, 121, 137
Function or Responsibility, 13, 109-122
Influence on Social Progress, 139-157
ICA Inquiry, vii-viii, 5-9, 10, 18, 19, 41, 45, 55, 77-78, 109
Liberty, 11, 13, 17, 92-108, 121, 145
Neutrality in Politics and Religion, 2, 3, 6, 8, 97-99, 105
Open and Voluntary Membership, 2, 6, 8, 23-24, 96, 105

Co-operative Retail Services, 152
Co-operative Union, Britain —

Co-operative Independent Commission, 62, 103
Model Rules, 13
Co-operative Wholesale Society, Britain, 25-26, 30, 51, 82
Correspondence Courses, 130
Cowden, Howard A., 19, 28
Credit Trading, 2, 6, 9, 41-43, 76, 119-120
Credit Unions, 21, 22, 27, 42, 43, 55, 78, 90, 119-120, 153
Dairy Co-operatives, 3, 29, 50, 66, 88, 101
Darwin, Charles, 21
Death Benefit, 87
Democracy, 2, 6, 8, 9, 11, 13, 16, 17, 19, 54-72, 93, 105, 106-107, 120, 121, 131, 132, 135, 137, 142-143, 144-146
Denmark —
Agricultural Co-operation, 47, 51, 129
Consumers Co-operatives, 151
Co-operative Marketing, 40-41
Co-operative Slaughterhouses, 89
Dairy Co-operatives, 101
Education, 129
Nordisk Andels-Export, 28
Nordisk Andelsforbund, 28
Derrion, Michel, 83
Discussion Groups, 130
Dividend on Surplus, 6, 8, 10-11, 44-45, 52, 73-74, 76-91, 105, 134, 135
Duttweiler, Gottlieb, 150

Economy, 10, 13, 17, 36-53
Education, 2, 6, 8, 9, 11, 13, 17, 88, 123-138, 145-146, 151
Elldin, Harald, 129-130
Employees, 62, 64-67, 68, 81, 82, 83, 86-87, 117, 119, 130, 144, 145
Equity, 13, 15, 17, 73-91, 95, 121, 137
Euro-Coop, 154
Europe —
Consumers Co-operatives, 84
Housing Co-operatives, 40
European Economic Community, 154

Farmers Co-operatives, 12-13, 21, 22, 23, 27, 29, 30, 32-33, 37, 38, 40, 41, 47, 49, 50, 51, 64, 65, 71, 78, 88-90, 95, 99, 101, 129, 154, 155
Fauquet, Dr Georges, 1, 9-10, 66, 72, 111, 121-122

Finland —
   KK, 9, 104
   Nordisk Andels-Export, 28
   Nordisk Andelsforbund, 28
   SOK, 9
Fourier, Charles, 14, 21, 43, 83, 86
France —
   Agricultural Co-operation, 29
   Confédération Générale, 86
   Coopération, 29, 83-84, 153
   Dividend on Purchases, 84
   Groupement National de la Coopération, France, 34, 153
   Members Meetings, 60
   National Federation of Consumers Co-operatives, vii-viii
   National Federation of Mutual Credit, 119
   National Printing Establishment, 66
   Remuneration Dispute, 87
   Union of Co-operators of Lorraine, 58-59
Freedom, 11, 13, 17, 92-108, 121, 145
Function or Responsibility, 13, 109-122

Galbraith, J.K., 39
Garratt, Roy, ix
Gasoline —
   Consumers Co-operative Association, 19, 26, 28
   Co-operative Gasoline Stations, 26-27
   International Co-operative Petroleum Association, 19, 28-29
Germany —
   Co-operation, 94, 98-99, 102, 151, 152-153
   Co-operative Legislation, 103
   Dividend on Turnover, 79
   Management, 62, 120
   Member Benefit Schemes, 45
   Members Meetings, 60
   Self-Service, 150
   West German Trade Union Bank, 151
   Workers Involvement in Policy Making, 66
Gide, Charles, 14, 15, 40, 93
Gray, J.C., 31
Greece —
   Co-operation, 152
   Syn-ka, 61-62
Groupement National de la Coopération, France, 34, 153
Guilds, Co-operative, 136

Hasselmann, Dr Erwin, 153
Hedberg, Anders, 131
Hire-Purchase, 42

Holland —
   Auction System, 23
   Consumers Co-operation, 98, 151
   International Co-operative Petroleum Association Processing Plant, 29

Holyoake, G.J., 5-6
Hot Springs Conference, 51
Housing Co-operatives, 37, 38, 40, 57, 90, 133, 153

Iceland —
   Nordisk Andels-Export, 28
   Nordisk Andelsforbund, 28
India —
   Co-operation, 69, 94
Insurance —
   Mutual Service Co-operative, USA, 70-71
   Nationwide, USA, 71
Interest on Share Capital, 6, 8, 76, 77-78, 79-91, 96
International Conference on Co-operative Thrift and Credit, 119-120
International Co-operative Alliance —
   Affiliation to, 3, 6, 7-8, 28, 69, 108, 149-150
   Congress, 4-5, 7, 9-10, 19, 150
   Co-operatives in Communist Countries, 3-4
   General, 28, 92, 155
   Inquiry into Application of Rochdale Principles, vii-viii, 5-9, 10, 18, 19, 41, 45, 55, 77-78, 109
   International Co-operative Congress 1895, 27
   Press and Education Conference, 146
   United Nations, 154
International Co-operative Petroleum Association, 19, 28-29
International Labour Organisation, 46, 48, 50, 147, 154, 155
Ireland —
   Co-operation, 3, 52
Italy —
   Co-operation, 98
   Labour Contracting Societies, 86-87

Jamaica —
   Waltham Land-purchase and Housing Society, 57
Jaures, Jean, 142

Johnson, Dr Samuel, 37

Keynes, John Maynard, 48
King, Dr William, 21, 24-25, 54, 76, 94,110
Kropotkin, Peter, 21

Labour Co-operatives, 21, 22, 23-24, 37, 47, 49, 64, 73, 75, 81-82, 83, 85-88, 153, 155-156
Laidlaw, Dr Alexander, 155
Liberty, 11, 13, 17, 92-108, 121, 145
Libraries, 128
Lincoln, Abraham, 55, 56

Malaysia —
  Jungle-Clearance and Rice Cultivation Project, 96
Management, 55-72, 104, 105, 119-120, 151
Mansbridge, Albert, xii
Marx, Karl, 64, 75
May, Henry J., vii, ix, xii, 4
Meetings, 55, 56-61, 67, 68, 70, 71, 77, 96, 120, 127, 132, 135
Members —
  Democracy, 2, 6, 8, 9, 11, 13, 16, 17, 19, 54-72, 93, 105, 106-107, 120, 121, 131, 132, 135, 137, 142-143, 144-146
  Education, 2, 6, 8, 9, 11, 13, 17, 88, 123-138, 145-146, 151
  General, 36, 49, 54, 79, 84, 90-91, 92, 94-102, 110-112, 119, 120-122
  Meetings, 55, 56-61, 67, 68, 70, 71, 77, 96, 120, 127, 132, 135
  Member Benefit Schemes, 44-45
  Open and Voluntary Membership, 2, 6, 8, 23-24, 96, 105
Mercer, Thomas William, vii, ix
Merger, 57, 103, 106, 134, 152
Morley, John, xiii

Neale, Vansittart, vii
Neurath, Dr Otto, 132
Neutrality in Politics and Religion, 2, 3, 6, 8, 97-99, 105
New Lanark, 20
New Zealand —
  Products, 30
Nordisk Andels-Export, 28
Nordisk Andelsforbund, 28
Norway —
  Nordisk Andels-Export, 28
  Nordisk Andelsforbund, 28

Officials, 55-63, 67, 86, 102, 105, 106, 119, 120, 122, 127, 134, 136, 137
Ollman, J.H., xi
Owen, Robert, 14, 17, 20, 54, 75, 83, 141-142
Pavitt, Laurie, xii
Pensions, 87
Pestalozzi, J.H., 123
Petroleum —
  Consumers Co-operative Association, 19, 26, 28
  Co-operative Gasoline Stations, 26-27
  International Co-operative Petroleum Association, 19, 28-29
Pioneers, Rochdale, vii-ix, 2, 4, 5-9, 10, 12, 14, 18-19, 24, 25, 40, 41, 42, 43, 45, 55, 56, 73, 75, 76, 77-78, 79, 80, 83, 84, 109, 110, 128, 132
Plunkett, Horace, 3, 13
Poisson, Ernest, 31
Political Neutrality, 2, 3, 6, 8, 97-99, 105
Portugal —
  Co-operation, 152
Press, Co-operative, 128, 129, 132, 133, 146
Prices, 38, 39, 41, 44, 50, 76, 79, 80, 83, 84, 85, 88, 89, 90, 91, 99
Productive Co-operatives, 21, 22, 23-24, 37, 47, 49, 64, 73, 75, 81-82, 83, 85-88, 153, 155-156
Profits, Division of, 6, 8, 10-11, 44-45, 52, 73-74, 76-91, 105, 134, 135
Propaganda, 125-127
Public Relations, 128
Publicity, 59, 100, 125
Purchasing Power, 22, 24, 25-26, 38, 39, 44, 50, 76, 99, 115
Purity of Goods, 40, 41, 50, 76, 88

Quality of Goods, 40, 41, 50, 76, 88

Rae, W. R., xii
Raiffeisen, Friedrich Wilhelm, 21, 78, 93
Regionalisation, 57, 103, 106
Religious Neutrality, 2, 3, 6, 8, 97-99, 105
Reserve Funds, 80, 83, 86, 105
Responsibility or Function, 13, 109-122
Rochdale Pioneers, vii-ix, 2, 4, 5-9, 10, 12, 14, 18-19, 24, 25, 40, 41, 42, 43, 45, 55, 56, 73, 75, 76, 77-78, 79, 80, 83, 84, 109, 110, 128, 132
Rousseau, J.J., 114

Rules, 1, 12, 13, 55, 56, 57, 77, 78, 84, 86, 96, 97, 99, 101, 104
Ruskin, John, 52
Russell, George, 52
Russia —
  Centrosoyus, 4
  Co-operation in, 3-4, 69
  Division of Surplus, 78
  Economy, 48
  Russian Revolution 1917, 3

Saint-Simon, Claude Henri, 21, 112-116
Salaries, 44, 74, 75-76, 81, 82, 87, 91, 115, 117-118, 148
Scandinavia —
  Agricultural Co-operation, 101
  Consumers Co-operation, 24
  Dividend, 85
  Nordisk Andels-Export, 28
  Nordisk Andelsforbund, 28
School Co-operatives, 128
Schulze-Delitzsch, Hermann, 21, 93
Scottish Co-operative Wholesale Society, 82
Self-Service, 150
Senior, Nassau, 74
Share Capital, 6, 8, 76, 77-78, 79-91, 96
Shaw, George Bernard, 141
Smith, Adam, 114,141
Social Dividend, 8, 45, 78
Soviet Union —
  Centrosoyus, 4
  Co-operation, 3-4, 69
  Division of Surplus, 78
  Economy, 48
  Russian Revolution 1917, 3
Spain —
  Co-operation, 152
Spencer, Herbert, 139, 140
Student Co-operatives, 128
Surplus, Division of, 6, 8, 10-11, 44-45, 52, 73-74, 76-91, 105, 134, 135
Sweden —
  Consumers Co-operation, 46, 150
  Dividend, 45
  Education, 129-131
  Kooperativa Förbundet, 129-131
  Nordisk Andels-Export, 28
  Nordisk Andelsforbund, 28
Switzerland —
  Consumers Co-operation, 24, 150, 151
  Consumers Co-operative Union VSK, 104-105

Dividend, 45, 85
Member Benefit Schemes, 44-45

Tanganyika —
  Coffee Unions, 27
Tawney, R.H., 114
Tayler, Dr J.B., 41
Thomas, Albert, 46-50, 59
Thompson, William, 21, 75
Trade Unions, 16, 22, 65, 74, 81, 95, 117, 118, 151

Training, 2, 6, 8, 9, 11, 13, 17, 88, 123-138, 145-146, 151

United Nations, 51, 154, 155
Unity, 10, 13, 15, 16, 18-35, 52, 72, 92, 97, 101, 102, 115, 142, 143
U.S.A. —
  Consumers Co-operative Association, 19, 26, 28
  Co-operative League of the USA, 19
  Credit Unions, 42
  Housing Co-operatives, 40, 153
  Insurance, 70-71
  Mutual Service Co-operative, 70-71
U.S.S.R. —
  Centrosoyus, 4
  Co-operation in, 3-4, 69
  Division of Surplus, 78
  Economy, 48
  Russian Revolution 1917, 3

Wages, 44, 74, 75-76, 81, 82, 87, 91, 115, 117-118, 148
Weights and Measures, 40, 41, 50, 76, 88
Whitman, Walt, 147
Wholesale Co-operation —
  Agriculture, 29
  Co-operative Wholesale Society, Britain, 25-26, 30, 51, 82
  Dividend, 45, 85
  General, 18, 27, 31
  Nordisk Andelsforbund, 28
  Scottish Co-operative Wholesale Society, 82
Workers, 62 64-67, 68, 81, 82, 83, 86-87, 117, 119, 130, 144, 145
Workers Co-operatives, 21, 22, 23-24, 37, 47, 49, 64, 73, 75, 81-82, 83, 85-88, 153, 155-156
Workers Educational Association, Britain, xii, 128-129

Youth Groups, 136

For a copy of our full Booklist of titles dealing with every aspect of Co-operation, please write to:

Holyoake Books
Holyoake House
Hanover Street
Manchester M60 0AS